AF663258

Professional Education in India

P. Satyanarayana
Lakshmi Mantha
C. Sesharatnam

SHIPRA

All rights reserved. No part of this publication may be reproduced or transmitted, in any form or by any means, without prior permission of the copyright holder and publisher.

The opinions and views expressed in this book are of the author(s) own and hence should not necessarily be attributed to the institution where s/he is employed and s/he is solely responsible for plagiarism & copyright issues, if any that arises.

₹ 995
US$ 40.00
ISBN: 978-93-88691-80-2

First Published in India in 2021

Professional Education in India

© Authors

Published by:
SHIPRA PUBLICATIONS
LG 18-19, Pankaj Central Market
I.P. Ext., Patparganj, Delhi 110092, India
Tel.: +91 11 2223 5152/6152; 96500 28065
E-mail: info@shiprapublication.com
www.shiprapublication.com

Contents

1 Engineering Education

Soon after the dawn of Independence, India launched a massive programme of development. Many large projects were undertaken to meet the needs of irrigation, power and flood control and to establish a basic industrial base for steel, machine tools, fertilisers, transportation, drugs and pharmaceuticals, petrochemicals, power equipment, etc. The country hardly had any industrial base or the infrastructure for the task of nation-building. A policy of planned development was adopted. However, one of the major problems faced by the country during the early years of planning was the acute shortage of trained technical manpower to meet the challenges. An ambitious programme of expansion of engineering education was undertaken to overcome the situation.

India has completed more than seven decades after Independence; during these years, the country has had 12 five year plans of development. The technology capacity of the nation, a key determinant of the pace, quality and quantum of economic and social growth has increased manifold. This has been possible on account of the corresponding quantitative and qualitative expansion of technical education.

Engineering education is a basic and essential input for national development and strengthening of the industry, economy and ultimately improving the quality of life of the people. It has made a significant contribution to India's economic development. The programmes which have advanced the country and diversified and augmented production since independence are largely because of the manpower produced by engineering institutions of the country.

In India, initially engineering education was based on the British model and emphasised the importance of engineering professional practice. After Independence, it has been constantly influenced by American education system in its content. The 20th century witnessed tremendous progress, and incredible developments took place in the field of engineering education. Technical education system is to produce trained manpower in adequate number for the economic and technological development of the country and to run its industries. It plays an important role for the economic and industrial growth, national development and international competitiveness. It imparts technical knowledge, study, and research, and facilitates technological transfer.

In India, engineering education at degree level is provided basically by five categories of Institutions:

- Institutions of national importance — IITs and NITs
- Technical universities
- Engineering departments, colleges in traditional universities
- State level government colleges
- Private engineering colleges.

The beginning of formal technical education in India can be traced back to the mid-19th century. The major policy initiatives in the pre-Independence period include appointment of Indian Universities Commission in 1902, adoption of Indian Education Policy resolution in 1904 and Governor General's Policy Statement of 1913 stressing the importance of technical education. The education establishment of IISc, Bangalore; Institute of Sugar, Textile and Leather Technology in Kanpur; NCE in Bengal in 1905 and industrial schools in several provinces were significant developments. Other developments such as:

- Constitution of technical education committee of the Central Advisory Board of Education in 1943
- Preparation of Sergeant Report of 1944
- Formation of the All India Council for Technical Education (AICTE) in 1945 by the Government of India facilitated the growth of technical education.

All India Council for Technical Education (AICTE)

The All India Council for Technical Education was set up in November 1945 as an apex organisation charged with the responsibility of planning and coordination in the development of technical education in India. The AICTE was vested with statutory authority for planning, formulation and maintenance of norms and standards, quality assurance through accreditation, funding in priority areas, monitoring and evaluation, maintaining parity of certification and awards and ensuring coordinated and integrated development and management of technical education in country.

The Government of India (Ministry of HRD) also constituted a national working group to look into the role of the AICTE in the context of proliferation of technical institutions, maintenance of standards and other related matters. The working group recommended that the AICTE be vested with necessary statutory authority for making it more effective which would consequently require restricting and strengthening with necessary infrastructure and operating mechanism.

The AICTE is responsible for the accreditation of all engineering institutions and it monitors the growth of technical education in relation to planned quantitative growth and proper maintenance of norms and standards. The National Board of Accreditation of the AICTE aims to bring standards of some of the programmes offered in technical institutions on par with programmes offered in the institutions in the USA and Europe by introducing a quality auditing system and establishing the datum for measuring the quality and excellence in engineering education. The accreditation exercise is very rigorous, has several inputs such as quality of teaching, level of research, faculty expertise, evaluation of teachers and standard of infrastructure and resources available at the institutions.

Major Committees

For analysis and improvement in technical education, many committees were set up. Some major committees and their recommendations are given below:

S.No.	Committee	Title	Year	Recommendations
1.	Sarkar Committee	Higher Technical Institutions for the post-War Industrial Development	1945	Setting up of Indian Institutes of Technology
2.	Thacker Committee	Postgraduate Engineering Education and Research	1959-61	Funding for 100 PhDs annually
3.	Nayudamma Committee	Postgraduate Education in Engineering and Technology	1979-80	PG Minimum Qualification for Industry R&D etc.
4.	Nayudamma Committee	IIT Review	1986	a. Greater flexibility in academic programme b. Focus on engineering research c. Faculty mobility

S.No.	Committee	Title	Year	Recommendations
5.	P Rama Rao Committee	Reshaping Postgraduate Education in Engineering and Technology	1995	a. 21 months MTech b. Increased scholarship amount c. Assured employment for MTech d. National Doctorial programme
6.	R A Mashelkar Committee	Strategic road map for academic excellence of future RECs	1998	Conversion of RECs into NITs with the status of a Deemed-to-be University and structural changes in governance
7.	U R Rao Committee	Revitalising the technical education	2003	a. Regional inequity to be removed b. Faculty shortage to be addressed c. Need for planning and coordination in working of the AICTE
8.	P Rama Rao Committee	IIT Review	2004	a. Increase UG output of IITs b. Fund infrastructure increase c. Add new IITs but maintain quality

After Independence, various educational commissions and committees recommended highly practical and research-oriented measures and development plans for technical education in the country. In 1945, Sarkar committee was appointed by the AICTE under the chairmanship of NR Sarkar. This committee recommended the establishment of higher technical education institutes known as IITs in order to meet post-War needs of engineers of higher level. These institutes aimed at providing excellence in Science and Engineering education.

UR Rao Committee Report

In 2002, a five-member committee headed by UR Rao, a prominent scientist and former chairman of the India Space Research Organisation, was established by the Ministry of Human Resources Development (MHRD) to review the performance of the AICTE. Submitted to the government in September 2003, the committee's report, Revitalizing

Technical Education, describes a technical sector that is expanding at an unsustainable level and is in drastic need of regulation to ensure that academic standards are improved.

When issued, the report sparked deep controversy and gained global coverage due to one of its more minor and tangential recommendations — cutting fees at the Indian Institutes of Management. The report's main findings and recommendations centre on the following areas:

- There are too many institutions due to unregulated growth, especially in the private sector
- Institutions are proliferating in geographical pockets, leading to oversupply in some markets and shortages in others
- Not enough qualified faculty, and not nearly enough doctorates coming through the system
- Weak quality assurance structures, especially accreditation procedures
- Lack of cooperation and interaction between industry and the classroom
- High levels of unemployment and underemployment among engineering graduates
- The graduate growth rate is far exceeding the economy's growth rate
- Colleges are not meeting the skilled manpower needs of industry
- Exorbitant tuition fees at many private colleges.

The first Indian Institute of Technology (IIT) was established on May 15, 1950 and was then called Eastern Higher Technical Institute. The present name "Indian Institute of Technology" was adopted just before its formal inauguration on August 18, 1951. A chain of IITs was later established in different parts of the country. These were declared as Indian Institutes of National Importance by an Act of Parliament 1961, amended in 1963.

In the year 2008, Ministry of Human Resources Development (MHRD) announced to open eight new IITs under XI Five Year Plan in different states of India and upgraded IT BHU as IIT to fulfill the demand of technical manpower of the country.

It was the dream of Jawaharlal Nehru, the first Prime Minister of India, to see India as a leader in science and technology. In 1955, Planning Commission appointed an Engineering Planning Commission (EPC) to undertake an overall assessment of the demand and supply position in respect of engineering personnel. To fulfill the demand of technical manpower, the Government of India started 17 Regional Engineering Colleges (RECs).

The REC system served well initially but as time passed, some state governments did not shoulder proper responsibility to steer the institutes in the right direction. Following the long standing demand for more IITs, the MHRD decided to upgrade all RECs to National Institutes of Technology (NITs) in 2002 with three new NITs. The Government of India introduced the National Institute of Technology Act, 2007 to bring 20 such Institutions within the ambit of the Act and to provide them with complete autonomy in their functioning.

By the end of 5th Plan (1974-79), there was considerable pressure for expansion of engineering institutions to fulfill the demand for technical manpower for sustainable development of the country, but governments were finding it difficult to make functional resources for the same. To handle the situation, some state governments especially Karnataka, Maharashtra, Tamil Nadu and Andhra Pradesh took a bold decision to permit private registered societies to establish and run engineering institutions on a self-financing basis and all these institutes were affiliated to the universities of the region or to the State Board of Technical Education. This type of private engineering institutions came in very large number but there was no effective mechanism to control their functioning nor was any systematic admission process. The above situation continued even after all Institutes were brought under the AICTE control and later the Supreme Court in its historical judgement defined the norms for admission and fee structure for all self-financing engineering institutions. After Supreme Court's decision, a large number of engineering institutions in different parts of the country were established and tried to satisfy the demand of technical manpower. Presently private engineering colleges running engineering courses both at degree and PG level are many.

Types of Engineering Institutions

1. Indian Institutes of Technology
2. National Institutes of Technology
3. Indian Institutes of Engineering Science and Technology
4. State Government-owned Engineering Universities
5. Indian Institutes of Information Technology
6. The Institution of Engineering (India)
7. Polytechnic Institutes.

Major Challenges

Engineering is one of the most coveted choices for students who wish to undergo undergraduate and postgraduate studies in India. There are thousands of engineering colleges in the country but only about 3000 of them have the necessary recognition. Fewer yet are deemed universities. Each year lakhs of students pass out of these colleges each with the hope of making it big, earning the lucrative sum each year. Most of them prefer to take up jobs in IT industry and in core engineering industries, but the top of engineering graduates either prefer to go abroad to pursue higher studies or take up management, seeking a job in the upper echelons of the corporate world. But do we have the opportunities necessary to employ these lakhs of students who hold an engineering degree? More importantly, are they equipped with the skills set necessary to guarantee them a prosperous career? Here comes the real challenge if a recent study is to be believed.

A Delhi-based employability assessment organisation, 'Aspiring Minds', recently conducted a study to assess the coding skills and programming logic of engineering students from computer and IT related branches. The result of the study may come as a shock to many. Aspiring Minds says that only about 4.7% of the students who are awarded engineering degrees from Indian colleges are capable of writing correct programming codes. About 60% of the candidates who were assessed by the study could not write any code at all.

Aspiring Minds undertook this study of 36,000 engineering students belonging to 500 colleges from different parts of India. Delhi engineers shared best scoring an average of 23.48 out of 100 on an automated programme created to test their skills and their practices. Mumbai, Bengaluru and Chennai engineers came next but the worst performances were of engineers from Kolkata and Hyderabad. This comes as a surprise since Hyderabad is reportedly the city that sends the most number of students to pursue Science, Technology, Engineering, Mathematics (STEM) degrees to the US. This is not the first time Aspiring Minds has undertaken such a study. Last year, the company undertook a study of 150,000 Engineering graduates from across the country but found only 7% of them possessing the skills suited for employment in core engineering jobs.

What or who is to blame? Experts believe that lack of quality education in the vast majority of the engineering colleges mushrooming across the country is to blame for this dismal state. Most private colleges charge greater amount as capitation fee and enroll students in mass without an adequate system for monitoring the quality of education and without exposure to particular challenges faced in the field.

Indian Engineering and Technology colleges — even the top ones such as IITs — do not rank among the top in the world. The curriculum followed in many streams such as in the case of software engineering is often outdated. Computer systems and software development is a dynamic field which demands constant adaptation to changes — something that education system fails to teach. Not only are our software professionals taught outdated programming languages, our engineers are asked to study old engineering and production techniques.

Aligning Ambitions with Capability

India harbours ambitions of becoming the manufacturing hub of the world. 'Make in India' is the Indian government flagship programme aimed at promoting manufacturing and services in India and inviting foreign investment. The bitter truth always remains that the quality of education and skills that we produce are not in sync with such colossal ambitions. As students and parents of students, we also need to realise that engineering is a career, a calling. More importantly, it is a set of skills one learns not merely a status symbol.

Recommendations of Chairman and Members of the AICTE Committee for Preparing Short and Medium Term Perspectives

The All India Council for Technical Education (AICTE) has been ably spearheading the planning, formulation, and dissemination of technical education across India. Over the years, it has undertaken several proactive steps for the growth of engineering education, maintenance of standards, and to keep the curricula current and relevant. While much has been accomplished, continuously changing expectations of the industry, society, and global stakeholder community owing to technology disruption, globalisation and changing student preferences call for a review of the engineering education in India. In this endeavour, the AICTE has constituted a Committee for Preparing Short and Medium Term Perspective Plan for Engineering Education in India.

The Committee studied the current state of engineering education in India. It has analysed AICTE data on engineering capacity and enrolment trends across the country, several analyst and associations' reports on the technologies, jobs and skills, and engineering education trends of the future. When interpreted along with expert opinions, we found several gap areas and issues that require immediate attention to improve the enrolment in various disciplines, employability of graduating students, capabilities of faculty, and the quality of pedagogy. These recommendations were included in the report titled: "Engineering Education in India: Short and Medium Term Perspectives."

Important Recommendations

Its important recommendations are given below:

1. Current (2017-18) capacity utilisation in undergraduate and post-graduate level is as low as 49.8%. (Capacity vs. Enrolment). Creating any further capacity is a big drain on investments since, at the very basic level, it involves the creation of physical infrastructure like buildings and lab infrastructure. We recommend that we do not create any new capacity starting from the academic year 2020. The creation of new capacity can be reviewed every two years after that.
2. While we take such a serious decision, we also recognise that there could be some applications in the pipeline for additional/new capacity applied in the last one or two years. These may be pending for want of some minor clearances. So, applications made in the current year and the past two years may be considered for starting institutions if the infrastructure is already in place.
3. We recommend that AICTE should take capacity utilisation as a key consideration while granting additional capacities in different states.
4. Traditional engineering disciplines such as Mechanical, Electrical, Civil and Electronics engineering have capacity utilisation around 40% as opposed to Computer Science and Engineering, Aerospace Engineering, Mechatronics being in the high 60%. This is a clear pointer that the demand lies in emerging technologies as opposed to traditional engineering. We recommend that no additional seats are approved in traditional engineering areas, but institutions need to be encouraged to convert current capacity in traditional disciplines to emerging new technologies.
5. The poor employability of engineering graduates is reflecting poorly on the faculty – shortage and quality, and pedagogy. It may be very important to take immediate steps to improve the quality of our teachers. a.) Competencies of the faculty need to be developed, especially in the areas of new-age technologies and research through rigorous faculty development programmes. Training of existing teachers at teachers training institutes, using quality improvement programmes (QIP) and using IIT/NIT faculty and infrastructure are some of the immediate interventions we recommend. b.) To bring about the desired change in the pedagogy in the immediate term, we recommend focused industry visits for faculty for hands-on

exposure to the latest technologies. Industry associations could be leveraged in facilitating this. c.) To improve pedagogy, we recommend engineering faculty to mandatorily have certification/diploma/degree in education.

6. Also, we may have to seek more technology interventions such as MOOCs to circumvent some of the constraints with faculty shortage and the quality of pedagogy. Students should be given more flexibility to use MOOCs in their core and optional curricula. Universities and autonomous institutions should be mandated to use MOOCs in the short term.
7. The low enrolment, lower placements, and low employability are causes for concern. Employment generation is very critical to a nation's economic development. While we are making certain recommendations on the role that academic institutes can play in improving the quality of education and indirectly contribute to the employment generation, all other stakeholders including government and industry should also start putting in place corrective measures to improve the employment generation.
8. As research becomes democratised, funds would need to be spent most optimally. Institutions need to build project management capabilities around research to ensure quick turnarounds, reduce cost and schedule overruns, and better collaborations across industry and academia.
9. Academic institutions have to continuously monitor the future skill requirements and make suitable changes to content and pedagogy so that the graduating students have the right capabilities for the job-in-demand. Hence, an institutional mechanism for periodic industry feedback on the technology upgradation and its impact on job roles needs to be put in place.
10. There is evidence to point out that the current industry-academia interaction requires improvement. We recommend the following interventions:
    a. Analytical tools should be used to understand the impact of various teaching methods and identify the best methods of executing coursework and apprenticeship — tightly integrate apprenticeship with pedagogy.
    b. Apprenticeship should be made mandatory on industry (in some ways it exists but needs rigorous implementation) and also progressively mandatory on educational institutions starting with 25% moving to 100% in five years.
    c. Two industry representatives to be part of the advisory board of each institution.

d. Deepening of industry-academia partnerships in applied research needs to be encouraged.
e. Establish 20 National Knowledge Functional Hubs (NKFH) as a pilot in the AICTE approved institutions to create an ecosystem of sustained industry-academia engagement.
f. We recommend that the AICTE takes the local industry ecosystem requirements (For instance, aerospace and IT engineering in Bengaluru vicinity, automotive in Chennai and Pune) into consideration while creating new capacities or increasing the existing capacities to deepen domain knowledge and to meet the industry requirements.
g. Simultaneously, we recommend that the AICTE balances this step with the national and global needs by introducing courses in new and disrupting technologies which are fungible across the country.

11. We have evidence to show that innovation, incubation and start-up ecosystem is lacking in educational institutions. As has been rightly recognised by the GOI, start-ups are a key driver for employment generation and wealth creation. Every educational institution should be mandated for the following: a.) Entrepreneurship should be a minor elective for undergraduates. b.) Tinkering labs similar to Atal Innovation Labs to be set up in every educational institution. c.) To promote start-ups, educational institutions need to set up incubation centres, mentoring clubs, and accelerator programmes.
12. Proxy indicators such as venture capital investments and engineering R&D investments by large companies for forecasting future technology shows a clear trend towards software and internet industries, healthcare services, and medical devices and semiconductor industry. They also clearly indicate that artificial intelligence (AI), internet of things (IoT) embedded SW, internet SW, mobility, analytics, and cloud are growing at a rapid pace as compared to traditional technologies. The results of the NASSCOM-BCG study and FICCI-NASSCOM-EY study also concur with this analysis.
    a. Across all engineering disciplines, we recommend that courses in these emerging technologies are made part of the curricula and made mandatory for computer science, electrical, and electronics engineering.
    b. Specifically, we recommend introducing undergraduate engineering programmes exclusively focused in AI, IoT, Blockchain, Robotics, Quantum Computing, Data

Sciences, Cyber Security, 3D Printing and Design, AR/VR (Indicative list).

c. Also, we recommend that we put greater focus on multi-disciplinary engineering courses, especially in computational biology, biotechnology, biomedical, mechatronics, space, aerospace, agriculture, and environmental engineering, by reducing the seats in conventional disciplines and converting some of the existing seats into these areas.

13. Research on future trends in education indicates student-centric learning needs to be given precedence. a.) We recommend students should be encouraged on design thinking and practical approaches to learning. b.) Students should also be made aware of real life socio-economic problems for them to solve using technology learnings. c.) Technology should be used for individual learning paths for each student (Education 4.0). d.) MHRD/AICTE should make investments in innovation in education and incubate education start-ups. e.) Open book examinations should be introduced wherever applicable to move students to higher order cognitive skills.
14. Finally, developing a perspective plan for engineering education should be an ongoing exercise. In the backdrop of rapidly-changing technology environment, engineering education needs continuous monitoring. We recommend that one of the industry bodies or a smaller group of industry bodies with the help of consultants who have a focus on education be tasked with this periodic planning exercise once every two years.

World Bank Workshop

On January 9, 2015 AICTE, CII and World Bank organised a workshop on "Implementing Strategies for Engineering Education in India towards 2025."

The workshop's comments on the performance of the vast majority of Engineering institutions in 2015 include:

- Largely, affiliated colleges are following the curriculum of universities;
- Only a small number of autonomous colleges are emerging;
- Focus of most of the Institutions undergraduate teaching and the postgraduate programmes is weak;
- Employers are not happy with engineering talent pool;
- Very little focus on research;

- Absence of academic framework to constantly respond to the changing needs of the economic environment;
- No serious engagement between education providers and employers;
- Lack of enterprise in character innovation mind set;
- Lack of systematic capacity building effort in education and research;
- Acceleration is more of a compliance rather than improvement tool;
- 95% to 100% revenue from government disbursement and/or student fees;
- No participation in regional development;
- Low key entrepreneurship promotion activities.

The workshop's goal was to come up with recommendations for how a significant number of engineering institutions would be able to improve the performance from the current dismal stage of development to the aspirational stage of high performing engineering Institutions over the next 10 years.

How high performing engineering institution should aspire to be in 2025?

- Institutions with full academic autonomy and adequate financial autonomy;
- Excellent teaching and Research intensive/research-led/research-informed Institution;
- Adaption of academic framework that is responsive to stakeholder's needs;
- More experiential practice-based curriculum creating relevant student experiences;
- Student learning outcomes in tune with employers' expectations;
- Strong link with industry in design development and delivery of the courses/programmes;
- Employers satisfied with the quality of the talent pool;
- Faculty training that is strongly linked to institutional processes and aspirations;
- Effective ICT technology adaption to enhance student learning and faculty competence;
- Strong post-graduate and research programmes;
- Enhanced capability for industry consultancy and IPR generation;
- Led by strong academic leaders and administrators who continually drive Institutional aspirations;

- At least 30% of expenditure met by revenue generated by other than government subsidies and/or student fees;
- Contributing to the regional socio-economic development through entrepreneurship and innovation activities;
- Centres of excellence in priority areas for the college.

The workshop suggested following five steps that can transform India's Engineering Education by 2025:

- Strengthen governance and leadership
- Improve quality of teaching, learning and research
- Faster stronger industry-institute collaborations
- Encourage innovation and entrepreneurships
- Make a concerted national initiative to improve engineering education.

Imperative Requirements

It is essential for engineering education system to keep itself updated with the global requirements in the present knowledge era. In view of the changing scenario, some of the imperative requirements for the engineering education system suggested by the Vice-Chancellor of Madan Mohan Malaviya University of Technology are as follows:

- Regulators of engineering education should evolve suitable framework for producing technical human resource with capability to meet the present-day challenges.
- All engineering education institutions should conduct their self-assessment in respect to the goals set by the regulators of engineering education.
- Establish suitable mechanism for creating a pool of good quality faculty human resources.
- Adoption of suitable teaching pedagogy for improvement in teaching methods and practices.
- Creating students-learning ambience for high quality classroom and laboratory teaching, which is better than the available digital content so that the student-teacher contact type education is strengthened.
- Update the curriculum so that it can help in achieving the present day goals of the engineering community.
- Enhance meaningful collaboration with industry for better interaction to improve the quality of engineering students.
- Creation of suitable IT enabled outreach system for strengthening engineering education.

- Supplement teaching content with relevant digital content in the routine teaching.
- Industry should adapt and rope in relevant academic Institutions for the regular interaction with academia and offer requisite opportunities to the budding technocrats – either through mutual consent or through certain legislative provisions.

Status of Engineering Colleges

At present in India there are more than 3500 degree engineering colleges. Out of these 20-25% is government engineering colleges and rest of the colleges are managed by private sector. At the initial stage up to 1970, the number of engineering students was nearly about 18,000 and now it has reached up to more than nine lakh. The growth of engineering colleges in India is reflected in the Table 1.1.

Table 1.1 Growth of Engineering Colleges in India

S.No.	Year	No. of Added Engineering Institutions	Cumulative No. of Engineering Institutions
1	Before 1960	100	110
2	1961-1970	35	145
3	1971-1980	13	158
4	1981-1990	179	337
5	1991-2000	441	778
6	2000-2010	2797	3575

The Table 1.1 states that in 1960, there were 100 institutions in India; by 1980 the number rose to 158. In the meantime, the AICTE has also drawn up model plans under estimates for an engineering college. New technical institutions were being established in accordance with the model. Till 2010. there were about 3575 engineering educational institutions functioning within annual intake of about 300 thousand students.

2 Architectural Education

Brief History

Any attempt to survey the brief history and the present status of architectural education in India must begin with a recognition that while the activity of architecture has been practised in India for centuries, its education was the responsibility of master craftsmen and passed along from one generation to another. The evolution of architecture as a profession is a relatively new phenomenon demanding a different educational approach and pedagogy. The problem is compounded by the fact that while the professional attitude is western import, the pedagogy requires issues of a distinct cultural identity and the resolution of tension between tradition and modern aspirations be integrally woven into the educational philosophy. Most schools have not come to grips with this problem and the pedagogical structure that arrived here from the West at the advent of the modern college level education has more or less remained.

The Sir J.J. School of Architecture (originally called the Government College of Art) in Bombay was the first modern school to introduce a structured course in architecture. In its initial years, the one architectural event to capture the imagination of the profession was the building of the Capital city of New Delhi by Lutyens. Many of the faculty, such as Claude Batley, while intellectually sympathetic to the need for an Indian identity, were, at the same time like Lutyens, grounded in the nineteenth century European Beaux Arts tradition and were fired by the grandeur of New Delhi.

The nineteenth century academic tradition had a technical bias in addition to the formal. Architectural form was a function of a resolution of forces acting upon it. August Choisy and Guadet of the École de Beaux Arts in Paris had laid the foundation of this attitude. While Lutyens and his disciples paid lip-service to Indian motifs, a thorough grounding in the art and craft of construction was always held to be a prerequisite for architectural training. This was reflected in the fact that the Bombay school had a strong technical component and all the schools that followed it, such as the Bengal Engineering College at Calcutta, Baroda's Kalabhavan, Delhi's Polytechnic, were primarily technical institutions with a department of architecture. Engineering and construction courses took up the lion's share of the curriculum.

Celebration of Technology at Kharagpur

With this background, the Indian Institute of Technology was founded soon after independence in collaboration with the Massachusetts Institute of Technology. The critical balance between classicism and technology which all schools were trying to maintain until then, tilted in favour of technology at Kharagpur. India's first Prime Minister Pandit Nehru's belief that a scientific temper and technology would transform India into a modem nation was in tune with MIT's own predisposition towards technology. Ever since the Second World War, MIT had been identified with a culture that held that technology will solve all mankind's problems. Thus, under MIT's guidance Kharagpur gave little importance to courses such as the history of architecture and even less to a study of Indian society, for technology was universal and transcended cultural differences.

It was not only the presence and importance given to technical courses that mattered in architecture, but the study of design too was also subjected to the same deterministic attitude and reduced to functional rationalism. A house was not only a machine to live in but its form was valid only to the extent of its capacity to answer to certain programmatic criteria. Paradoxically, this created an interesting situation; late Prof. Kurula Varkey, a Kharagpur alumnus was to remark that it was this absence of humanities and liberal arts component in their education that led some of the more sensitive students to search, on their own, for the values and ideas that inform architecture.

Modernism at Baroda

The School at Baroda was started before independence and was initially an affiliate of the School at Bombay. In 1949, the MS University of Baroda was established and the technical departments of Kalabhavan were converted to the faculty of Technology and Engineering. Interestingly, the Department of Architecture became a part of the newly established and unique Faculty of Fine Arts. The diploma course, originally offered as part of the Kalabhavan programme, was upgraded a few years later to a full-fledged B. Arch. degree course under the able leadership of Professor M. B. Dave, a one-time associate of Claude Batley.

Professor Dave ensured that the curriculum include courses in humanities (he himself taught history of architecture) and the Beaux Arts emphasis on the 'making of architecture', that is, one's ability to put together a building properly, the tectonics of architecture was incorporated in the pedagogy. Besides, the university had always had an excellent liberal arts programme with a number of prominent personalities actively engaged in exploring ideas of modernity. In those early years when the university was relatively small and interaction between departments was still possible, students of architecture would find themselves in the company of students from the literature, philosophy and social science departments.

These lateral exposures made sure that the architecture faculty's preoccupation with classicism and technology was supplemented with at least some, albeit not well-formed, questions of relevance and ideology though they were still conceived in terms of neo-rationalism. However, there was a conspicuous absence of anti-historicist monumentality in student projects done at that time, and this promised to be a significant departure and set the school apart from others.

Unfortunately, this phase lasted only a few years. Had the Department of Architecture remained with the Faculty of Fine Arts its history would probably have been different. It so happened that the teachers of the Department, against the wishes of Professor Dave, voted to be a part of the Faculty of Technology and Engineering in the early '60s. This arrangement has remained ever since. Successive deans of the larger faculty, who were themselves engineers, failed to understand the unique blend of technology, humanities and aesthetics in architecture and successfully subjected the Department to the utilitarian, problem-solving culture of the technical disciplines with all its attendant problems. Successors to Professor Dave, unfortunately, were not able to resist this pressure nor have they been able to infuse a sense of direction and purpose to the School.

Decline and its Reasons

In recent years universities, like all other institutions, have come under tremendous political and regional pressures and the first casualty is the 'universal' character of the university. Where 'Pursuit of Excellence' should be the guiding motto, we have a preoccupation with status quo. Three decisions which most universities have made are of interest to us. One, following the political dictate of the State governments, is to limit the admission to the schools of architecture (as part of engineering units) to the students of the respective state only, as a way of ensuring the regional interest. The second decision concerns the selection of the heads of departments. This is usually done through a system of rotation. Selection is almost always made on the basis of seniority rather than leadership quality and a vision for the school. And the third decision automatically gives tenure to a teacher after he or she completes two years without making waves. As a result, faculty often does not have either the peer pressure to upgrade themselves or the motivation to do so. This absence of accountability is especially acute in government-run colleges. After a few years, seniority ensures advancement and even leadership. These factors though have played havoc with the standards of the schools.

Council of Architecture

The Council of Architecture was established in the early seventies as a statutory body with a view to oversee both the profession and the education of architects. With the expansion of the profession and proliferation of schools of architecture, a regulatory mechanism was necessary. The Council laid down certain norms of minimum facilities, procedures and courses that each school has to follow and instituted periodic inspection to ensure adherence. Though primarily mandated to oversee and regulate the profession, the Council was also given responsibility to regulate the education at undergraduate level.

In early eighties, another statutory body came into being the All India Council of Technical Education (AICTE) with a mandate to regulate all technical education systems in the country. By this time the popular psyche had been conditioned to consider architecture as a technical discipline as opposed to a design discipline and it naturally came under the purview of AICTE. But this created a strange situation with two statutory bodies looking at architecture. This has now been resolved with a Memorandum of Understanding between the two Councils reached whereby part of the responsibility of setting the minimum curricular standards has been given to the Council of Architecture, though the AICTE still retains a larger control with powers for financial dispersal and approval for Post Graduate programmes.

No doubt the Council of Architecture was instituted with good intentions. It has resulted in a certain awareness of a regulatory body and procedures and has made the schools answerable to a body other than university authorities. However, while the Council does ensure the minimum level of performance, it has not been able to effectively guide or motivate schools of architecture to go beyond the minimum. The simple reason is that the Council has to draw from the available pool of professionals and school administrators to define the minimum standards and conduct periodic inspections. The limitation of this resource becomes the shortcoming of the Council. Barring a few notable exceptions, most of the people connected with the academic side of the Council are prone to thinking of schools of architecture as extensions of the profession.

Critical Energy at Ahmedabad

The School of Architecture at Ahmedabad is an exception to the above trend. By deliberately and studiously avoiding the affiliation with a university, (recently the school has been forced by the Council to affiliate with the North Gujarat University) Ahmedabad has maintained academic and administrative autonomy and with an innovative programme has emerged, in a short span of twenty five years, as a centre of excellence with international recognition.

The School started in 1962 under the aegis of the Ahmedabad Education Society and was actively supported and encouraged by Kasturbhai Lalbhai, a leading industrialist and philanthropist of the city. The School's initial direction was set by the able troika of architect BV Doshi, Dr Rasvihari Vakil and Bernard Kohn who, on the recommendation of Louis Kahn left a teaching position at Yale University to come to Ahmedabad.

The School broke away from the conventional fixed course structure which was prevalent at the time and instead adapted a more open curriculum with many elective courses. It also incorporated two important components: a 'related study programme' requiring students to measure-draw important historical buildings, and a 'thesis programme' which requires that each undergraduate student writes a research dissertation on a subject of his/her choice. Now a few schools have incorporated such programmes but for a long time this was the only school with such a programme for undergraduate students. With a tentative beginning the school has now built up an impressive collection of theses on a variety of subjects, as well as a portfolio of documentation on Indian architecture

Interestingly, in the initial years, there was no programme of teaching history and theory of architecture at Ahmedabad. Whatever history was taught was more akin to archeology than history. However, almost all the design faculty referred to historical examples while reviewing design projects. This not only whetted students' appetite for history, but the subject acquired an immediate relevance to the present.

Over the years the School has grown into a full campus with several related institutions. The School of Architecture, though, continues to be its main identifying institution and is recognised as a cultural force in the city. It is a measure of its success that a number of European and American schools now seek exchange programmes with Ahmedabad

A few other independent schools have been recently started. Notable among these are the Academy of Architecture at Bombay, the Habitat School at Delhi and the one at Hassan in Karnataka.

Architecture and its Associates Programmes

A. Various Programmes on Architecture Education at Diploma Level
   1) Diploma in Architecture Assistantship 3 years
   2) Diploma in Interior Designing 1 year, 2 years, 3 years
   3) Diploma in Building Construction and Management 2 years and 3 years.

B. Various Programmes on Architecture Education at Graduation Level
   1) B. Arch. (Construction and Management)
   2) B. Arch. (Interior Design)
   3) B. Arch. (Computer Application)
   4) B. Arch. (Building Construction and Technology).

C. Various Programmes on Architecture Education at Post-Graduation Level
   1) M. Arch. (Architecture Design)
   2) M. Arch. (Environmental Architecture)
   3) M. Arch. (Construction Project Management)
   4) M. Arch. (Valuation)
   5) M. Arch. (Sustainable Architecture)
   6) M. Arch. (Architecture Education)
   7) M. Arch. (Landscape Architecture)
   8) M. Arch. (Digital Architecture)
   9) M. Arch. (Industrial Architecture) {M. Design}
   10) M. Arch. (Urban Design)
   11) M. Arch. (Real Estate Management)
   12) M. Arch. (Housing)
   13) M. Arch. (Architecture Conservation)
   14) M. Arch. (Building services)
   15) M. Arch. (Recreational Architecture)
   16) M. Arch. (Medical Architecture)
   17) M. Arch. (Urban Regeneration)
   18) M. Ekistics.

D. Various Certificate Courses
   1) Course offered by various CADD Centres: 1, 2 and 3 year
   2) Certificate Courses on Architecture Education: 3 years.

E. Student Awareness Programmes
   1) Career and Counselling Programmes
   2) Various Students Exchange Programmes
   3) Architecture Awareness Competitions.

Various Organisations which Work on Architecture Awareness

1) C.O.A. (Council of Architecture)
2) N.A.S.A. (National Association of Student of Architecture)
3) N.I.A.S.A. (National Institute of Advanced Studies in Architecture)
4) I.I.A. (Indian Institute of Architects)
5) H.U.D.C.O. (Housing and Urban Development Corporation)
6) C.B.R.I. (Central Building Research Institute)
7) C.A.A. (Commonwealth Association of Architects)
8) R. I B A. (Royal Institute of British Architects)
9) I.A.H.H. (International Association of Humane Habitat)
10) ETHOS
11) G.B.C. (Indian Green Building Council)
12) L.E.E.D. (Leadership in Energy and Environmental Design)
13) G.R.I.H.A. (Green Rating for Integrated Habitat Assessment)
14) I.N.T.A.C.H. (Indian National Trust for Art and Cultural Heritage)
15) A.S.I. (Archaeological Survey of India)
16) HABITAT WORLD
17) T.E.R.I.
18) Delhi Heritage Walks.

Table 2.1 Year wise Registration of Architects

S. No.	Year	No. of Architects
1	2017	2991
2	2016	7306
3	2015	7001
4	2014	4251
5	2013	4001
6	2012	3898
7	2011	3412
8	2010	4034
9	2009	3042
10	2008	2316
11	2007	2333
12	2006	1943
13	2005	2311
14	2004	2265
15	2003	2200
16	2002	1812
Total		**55,116**

Table 2.2 State wise Architects

S. No.	State Name	No. of Architects
1	Andaman and Nicobar Islands	22
2	Andhra Pradesh	753
3	Arunachal Pradesh	40
4	Assam	442
5	Bihar	445
6	Chandigarh	568
7	Chhattisgarh	554
8	Dadra and Nagar Haveli	14
9	Daman and Diu	21
10	Delhi	6467
11	Goa	550
12	Gujarat	3329
13	Haryana	2253
14	Himachal Pradesh	321
15	Jammu and Kashmir	241
16	Jharkhand	333
17	Karnataka	4579
18	Kerala	2870
19	Lakshadweep	3
20	Madhya Pradesh	1580
21	Maharashtra	18079
22	Manipur	75
23	Meghalaya	92
24	Mizoram	57
25	Nagaland	35
26	Odisha	686
27	Puducherry	114
28	Punjab	1190
29	Rajasthan	1417
30	Sikkim	54
31	Tamil Nadu	5205
32	Telangana	2389
33	Tripura	22
34	Uttar Pradesh	4175
35	Uttarakhand	443
36	West Bengal	1572
	Total	**60992**

Source: Council of Architecture-website (as on 19.06.2017)

Top 10 Architecture Colleges in India (2019)

1. School of Planning and Architecture, Delhi
2. IIT, Kharagpur
3. Sir JJ college of Architecture, Mumbai
4. Birla Institute of Technology, Mysore
5. Jadavpur University, Kolkata
6. Chandigarh College of Architecture, Chandigarh
7. Jamia Milia Islamia, Delhi
8. NIT, Tiruchirappalli
9. Centre for Environmental Planning and Technology, Ahmedabad
10. Manipal Institute of Technology, Manipal

Required Changes

To find the required changes in Architectural Education, the purpose of Architectural Education must be understood. An understanding is needed on the historical concept on why architectural studies were kept distinctly different from technical education, why a separate identity needed, and why the architecture education requires a longer duration of study.

All the challenges that persist in our education system today are not new and should not be treated as a major cause of worry. The Council is working with Professionals and the Other Decision Makers and Colleges to regulate and weed out the ineffective teaching shops that give precedence to Architectural Institutes as Commercial Entities.

The Council has already created a framework in the form of Minimum Standards of Architectural Education. It covers 75% of required study to gain education to become an architect. It gives freedom to the colleges to orient the course as per their own philosophy by choosing the subjects in the balance 25% course. The first stage covers 2880 contact periods, out of which 570 periods are left to the discretion of the institute. So, further regulation will not lead to the betterment or renewal of the profession.

As indicated in the 2004 approach paper by Prem Chandavarkar, a vision document by the Architectural Institute would be a good way forward for any Architectural Institute. Such vision documents would allow the teachers to equip themselves and prepare students who would be geared up to meet the expectations of becoming problem-solvers.

Any such vision paper is not expected to be a static document that remains on institutes' websites but should be reflective of the problems the society or the country faces. Every few years based on prevailing conditions it should be changed. For example, the focus of the country is "Housing for All". Immense opportunities exist today, and challenges of achieving the vision lie in working out a solution that would allow quick and standardised construction at the lowest possible cost.

Another example to illustrate and reinforce the concept would be a vision document that the Academic Council of Institute could create would be on Infrastructure or Port Development or Rural Development or Urban Infrastructure.

The other required changes that are required is to reduce the Gestation Period in Learning. This can be achieved by integrating the Academia into Profession. This can be understood in the following scenario. Every practising architect has limited or non-existent time devoted to research. As a result, very frequently, an architect only offers to his/her client a solution that has been adopted earlier. This leads to stagnation in idea, and profession does not evolve over time. In such a scenario, whenever a foreign architect brings a fresh new idea, he is seen as a solution provider by Indian Client. Although the Council is working towards regulating the practice of architecture by foreign architects, but it is a reality and need that Indian Architects create their own identity and devote time to research to cater to such need. This is where the Academia can step in and offer its expertise to the profession.

Till date a standardised architectural contract remains undefined. All the contracts are made by Clients' Legal and Finance Teams. They are designed to take care of client needs. Institutes can research the needs of the profession and create framework documents. Such integration of profession and academia will allow the profession to renew itself and redraw its boundary with every step.

Conclusion

It is the mandate of Council of Architecture to be an enabler and it relies on the Academia and Professionals to give its inputs to frame the Minimum Formal Education required to educate a student to gain qualifications adequate enough to become an Architect.

This means that its task is not to coerce Architectural Colleges into following a central thought, but it encourages them to become centers of excellence and expects the profession to renew itself with the needs of the society. The problems that plague the profession should not cause us to divert majority of the energy, but the energies should be focused in availing the opportunities that present themselves.

3 Medical Education

Medical Education in Ancient India

The medical education in India can be traced back to the era of Charaka and Sushrutha who had their own doctrines in treating and teaching indigenous system of Medicine in ancient India. The formal training of Indians in Medical Science has started at the time of British rule in India where initial emphasis was given to establish the medical schools that provide instructions to students in native languages. Medical Colleges in Madras, Bombay, and Calcutta were established with the objective to afford better means of instruction in Medicine and Surgery to the Indo-British and native youths, entering the medical branch of the service in the presidency. Later on, several institutions to train Indian youths in indigenous system of medicine such as Ayurveda, Unani, Homeopathy, and Siddha were established throughout the country.

Even after the independence, the medical education in India did not come out of colonial yoke. Most of our medical schools still felt comfortable with western mode of instruction rather than tailoring the curriculum to the local needs. In the mid-1970s, the Shrivastav Committee advocated reorientation of medical education by national priorities and needs. In 1986, the Bajaj Committee called for the establishment of an educational commission for health sciences. It also noted that medical school faculty, though efficient in their clinical specialties, were deficient as educators. In order to meet the societal need of doctors, larger number of government and private medical colleges were established across the country. These medical colleges have been successful in creating the doctors who could cure the diseases but failed to provide comprehensive health care which includes preventive, promotive, curative, and rehabilitative services to the people who are in need of the health care services. Over a period of time, medical education in India has turned out to be a business sector, with competitive pricing for providing basic and specialised certification. Establishment of the Medical

Council of India (MCI) as a statutory body for the maintenance of uniform standards of medical education, both undergraduate and postgraduate, was one of the welcome steps to ensure check on basic minimum requirements for the establishment and running of undergraduate and postgraduate programmes in Medicine. There is also a strong criticism that the statutory body itself hinders the flexibility of offering medical education in the country through its stringent rules and regulations.

Present Medical Education

The state of medical education in India is at crossroads. It represents a scenario marked by rhetoric wishful thinking rather than concrete steps in the right direction. Sticking on to the age-old curricula which was developed more than 100 years ago, which compartmentalises the medical disciplines rather than giving holistic understanding of the subject, is the root cause for these problems. Every academician and governing authority in all possible academic forums advocate the need for bringing rampant curriculum reforms in medical education by tailoring it to the current needs and demands, but when it comes to action, we are still at ground zero.

Apart from curriculum, we still believe that the role of a medical teacher is like a sage on the stage rather than guide by the side. We often want our students to sit in the class like the rat which is a passive and motivation-free recipient of stimuli and listen to the lectures of an elated faculty member for hours together and feel scared to interact with him. There is a need that this scene in classrooms should change in such a way that the teacher should act as a facilitator and allow students to learn by themselves through active involvement based on the principle of cooperative learning. Thus, the classrooms should become the platforms for two-way sharing of ideas and thoughts between teachers and students with larger scope for healthy debate and dialogues.

The serious concern about the current syllabus is that it is stuffed with a lot of knowledge component, in medical education terms, cognitive domain with little psychomotor domain (clinical skills) with almost no emphasis on affective domain (attitude). The most essential elements of affective domain such as empathy, professionalism, altruism, communication skills, ethics, and humanities are not covered in anyways in the syllabus. Some people argue that these are the behavioural attributes which cannot be formally taught in the medical school thus the student needs to be adapting them by observing their teachers, this was called as "hidden curriculum". Considering the current day's incidences such as assault on doctors, professional negligence, violence in clinical setting force us to somehow inculcate them in the current system of medical education. Coming to the psychomotor domain, are we confident enough to say that any student graduated from our institution can independently perform any clinical task in any health care setting (primary, secondary and tertiary)? The students who are taught in the tertiary care hospital feel less competent to work in the resource-limited primary care settings. Thus, we need to ensure the graduate should be equipped with some basic competencies to practise his clinical skills in a proficient manner in a given setting in an independent way; these are called entrustable professional activities (EPA).

The current system of assessment is a mockery of assessment in the real sense. The learning of student for the whole academic year is judged based on his/her performance in single summative theory examination and a viva voce of three minutes. Cannot we have a formative assessment of the student on his performance on day-to-day basis and certify him based on his level of achievement of desired competencies at the end of academic year? The assessment techniques for practical examinations we use are quite subjective and lack reliability. The marks awarded by the examiner are most commonly based on his/her subjective interpretation of the concepts. Thus, there is a need to make assessment more objective by introducing the concepts of objective structured practical and clinical examinations. The student who performs extremely well in controlled examination setting may not do the same way in real-world scenario and vice versa. Thus, we need to take the assessment at workplace and certify the competency of the student based on his performance in the actual clinical setting; this is called workplace-based assessment.

The loop of education gets completed with the mechanism of giving and receiving feedback. How many medical teachers give proper and timely feedback to the students? And receive the feedback from them on the mode of teaching and curriculum? How many of our institutions get feedback from the community on the ultimate product we have produced (doctors) for their benefit? Thus, we need to establish an efficient feedback circuit which addresses the concern of each of the stakeholder in the education system.

After a series of consultations and deliberations, the MCI has come up with a set of core competencies for an Indian Medical Graduate.

1. Clinician
2. Life-long learner
3. Communicator
4. Leader
5. Professionalism.

Under these core competencies, several sub-competencies are defined to bring out a quality product — Indian Medical Graduate. There is a due emphasis given on introducing a module on attitudinal, ethics, and communications skills for the medical students from the day they entre medical school. Currently, MCI Regional Centres across the country are training the faculty members on the implementation of this module. Another major reform taken up by the MCI is the introduction of basic course workshops on educational technologies for all the teachers in the medical colleges and advanced course in medical education for the selected faculty. These courses empower the medical teachers with adequate knowledge and skills toward designing the curriculum, bring innovations in teaching-learning methods and assessment techniques.

The experiments in the West have proved that student-centered, outcome-based mode of medical education is more effective than the current method we follow, which is teacher-centered and content based. This method of medical education which keeps student as a basic unit and his learning outcomes or competencies as the endpoints is popularly known as competency-based medical education (CBME). CBME is a paradigm shift where the curriculum is designed based on the community/societal needs. The learning outcomes or competencies are tailored to these needs. The teaching-learning methods and assessment are integrated by dividing the boundaries between specialties. For example, if the student has to learn about hypertension as a topic he will have to learn, anatomy of heart and blood vessels (anatomy), physiology of circulation (physiology), pathogenesis of hypertension (pathology), epidemiology of the condition (community medicine), antihypertensive medications (pharmacology), and management of the condition (general medicine). In the current system of medical education, all these components of hypertension are compartmentalized, and student learns them separately across different years of MBBS programme and undergoes assessment accordingly. However, in case of CBME, the teaching and assessment will get integrated across all these specialties, and the student learns hypertension as a whole in a comprehensive manner. The assessment will also take place accordingly.

In CBME, the teacher will be very clear about what has to be taught, and the student is also aware of what is expected out of him/her after undergoing the learning exercise. The curriculum will set the goal of a learning programme, defines different roles to the stakeholders involved, designs a set of competencies, divides the competencies into several sub-competencies, specifies the learning objectives to fulfill them, tailors teaching-learning methods accordingly and also plans assessment tools to know whether the student has achieved the outcomes or not.

A Sample Framework of Competency Based Medical Education (CBME)

The role of the teacher in CBME is more of facilitating the learning of students by being guide by the side. More of small group teaching methods, self-directed learning, cooperative learning methods, and communities of practice are encouraged rather than didactic lectures and notes taking. The teachers have to plan their sessions to be more interactive and encourage student to clear their concepts as and when required. Giving feedback on the learning of students is a very important aspect of CBME. The teachers should acquire essential knowledge and skills pertaining to various methods of providing timely, formative, constructive, balanced, specific, and goal-oriented feedback to the students.

Assessment in CBME is a very interesting business. The knowledge, attitude, and skills of the student are assessed on regular basis (formative assessment), and specific feedback is given in order to improvise further. The student undergoes several such assessments before he takes certification examination. In the final (summative) assessment, due weightage is given to the performance of student in the formative assessments. The techniques of assessment of student are more objective, structured, reliable, and valid compared to the traditional tools which are more subjective in nature. These tools include objective-structured practical examination, objective-structured clinical examination and record, multisource feedback, mini-clinical evaluation exercise (Mini-CEX), and mini-peer assessment tool. Most of these tools are task-oriented and can be performed at the workplace itself. Thus, they are also known as workplace-based assessment tools. Most of these tools are available in open source, but when any institution chooses to use them for their students; they need to be benchmarked and standardised based on the local needs.

At the end of educational experience, the student should be able to carry out any clinical task independently with adequate accuracy, confidence, and efficiency without any assistance from the facilitators/teachers at a given point of health care. These set of professional activities which the graduated student is entrusted to perform at the end of the programme are called EPA (e.g., conducting a normal vaginal delivery). Now, most of the medical schools in the West are providing medical education to the students keeping these EPAs as the basic endpoints.

The CBME also faces semi-challenges. These include:

- Lack of training among medical faculty on designing and implementing the CBME curriculum
- Higher student-to-teacher ratio in medical colleges

- Lack of time
- The absence of adequate infrastructure to teach students in small groups and conduct multiple assessments
- Lack of commitment among managements to bring changes in the existing system
- Inertia among faculty and students for change
- It is not a mandate from the regulatory authority (like MCI).

All these challenges can be easily overcome by motivating faculty to undergo faculty development programmes and bringing in policy changes from the regulatory bodies.

"Change is the only constant." The system of medical education needs to adapt itself to adapt the rapid changes taking place in the area of medical science and health care. We need to move away from traditional, teacher-centered, content-oriented mode of education to the student-centered, and outcome-oriented medical education system. There is a need to adapt CBME through adequate faculty training and stakeholder participation. In order to make an Indian Medical graduate into an International Medical Graduate, the model of medical education needs to undergo a paradigm shift.

National Medical Commission (NMC)

Medical Council of India (MCI), apex regulatory body of medical education and profession, was dissolved in 2010 following corruption charges against its President by the Central Bureau of Investigation (CBI). The Central Government brought the National Medical Commission Bill, 2019, the biggest reform in the history of medical education in India. The NMC Bill was passed by Lok Sabha on July 29, 2019 and by Rajya Sabha on August 1, 2019. It got assent of the President of India on August 8, 2019.

NMC is an Act to provide for a medical education system:

- That improves access to quality and affordable medical education, ensures availability of adequate and high-quality medical professionals in all parts of the country.
- That promotes equitable and universal healthcare that encourages community health perspective and makes services of medical professionals accessible to all the citizens.
- That promotes national health goals.
- That encourages medical professionals to adopt latest medical research in their work and to contribute to research.
- That has an objective periodic and transparent assessment of medical institutions and facilitates maintenance of a medical

register for India and enforces high ethical standards in all aspects of medical services.
- That is flexible to adapt to changing needs and has an effective grievance redressal mechanism and for matters connected therewith or incidental thereto.

Powers and Functions of the NMC: The Commission shall perform the following functions, namely

a Lay down policies for maintaining a high quality and high standards in medical education.
b Lay down policies for regulating medical institutions, medical research and medical professionals,
c Assess the requirements in health care, including human resources for health and health care infrastructure and develop a roadmap for meeting such requirements,
d Promote, coordinate and frame guidelines and lay down policies by making necessary regulations for the proper functioning of the Commission, the Autonomous Boards and the State Medical Councils.
e Ensure coordination among the Autonomous Boards.
f Take such measures as ensure compliance by the State Medical Councils of the guidelines framed and regulations made under this Act for their effective functioning under this Act.
g Exercise appellate jurisdiction with respect to the decisions of the Autonomous Boards.
h Lay down policies and codes to ensure observance of professional ethics in medical profession and to promote ethical conduct during the provision of care by medical practitioners.
i Frame guidelines for determination of fees and all other charges in respect of fifty per cent of seats in private medical institutions and deemed-to-be universities which are governed under the provisions of this Act.
j Exercise such other powers and perform such other functions as may be prescribed.

The Medical Advisory Council

The Central Government shall constitute an advisory body to be known as the Medical Advisory Council.

Functions of the Medical Advisory Council

1 The Council shall be the primary platform through which the States and Union territories may put forth their views and concerns before the Commission.

2 The Council shall advise the Commission on measures to determine and maintain, and to coordinate maintenance of the minimum standards in all matters relating to medical education, training and research.
3 The Council shall advise the Commission on measures to enhance equitable access to medical education.

National Examination

National Eligibility-cum-Entrance Test: There shall be a uniform National Eligibility-cum Entrance Test for admission to the undergraduate and postgraduate super-specialty medical education in all medical institutions. The National Eligibility-cum-Entrance Test will be conducted in English and in other languages.

National Exit Test (NEXT): A common final year undergraduate medical examination, to be known as the National Exit Test shall be held for granting license to practise medicine as medical practitioners and for enrolment in the State Register or the National Register.

Any person with a foreign medical qualification shall have to qualify National Exit Test for the purpose of obtaining licence to practise medicine as medical practitioner and for enrolment in the State Register or the National Register. The National Exit Test shall be the basis for admission to the postgraduate broad based-specialty medical education in medical institutions.

Autonomous Boards

The Central Government shall constitute the following Autonomous Boards, under the overall supervision of the NMC, to perform the functions assigned to such Boards.

Contentious Issues Regarding National Medical Commission

The entire medical community: Under graduate and Post-graduate students, residents, junior doctors, consultants and the teachers of the medical institutions — as well as the leaders of the opposition parties are opposing the proposed provisions of the Act. Although, the NMC Act has now become a law, it has not been notified by the Central government. The major issues of contention are the following:

- Entire Organisational Structure is dominated by nominations
- Giving freehand to Private medical Colleges in terms of determination of fees
- Allowing the Community Health Providers to prescribe allopathic medicines.

Scourge that Afflicts Medical Education

On June 11, 2008, a 32-year-old doctor overdosed herself with anesthesia at the college quarters and died. Her final hand-written suicide note outlines exorbitant fees hiked arbitrarily, non-payment of full stipend and a resulting debt trap, as reasons that forced her decision.

Smriti's father Kishore speaks of his bright young daughter who had completed her MBBS from government-run Gandhi Medical College (Bhopal) and secured a merit-based seat in Index Medical College through the common NEET exam.

The college demanded annual fees of ₹8,55,000 plus 2,00,000 for hostel, he says, adding that he managed a loan of ₹35 lakhs for Smriti's education.

"However, when we were paying the fees, an additional 2,00,000 was demanded," alleges Kishore (60), a retired bank employee.

Mid-session, the college hiked the tuition fee from ₹8,55,000 to 9,90,000 and told the students to pay the difference of ₹1,35,000 per year for three years, he alleges. "Students, including Smriti, moved the court and despite repeated High Court orders to not hike fees, the college kept demanding enhanced fees, an additional ₹4,05,000 over the course of three years," says Kishore.

Close to a month later, the police registered a first information report against Suresh Bhadoriya, Chairman of the Index group which owns the medical college and Dr. K.K. Khan, Head of Department, Anesthesiology, both of whom Smriti had held responsible for abetting her suicide.

Efforts to contact college authorities did not elicit a response.

The incident is a murky reminder of the massively unregulated business of private medical education across the country.

The last decade has seen medical schools in India increase from 256 in 2006 to 479 in 2017, of which 259 are privately owned and managed.

The Union Health Ministry barred 82 medical colleges from taking admissions in 2018-19, on the ground of inadequate infrastructure and faculty. Twelve of these were government-run, the remaining 70 being privately-owned.

Far from being a social mission, medical education is seen as a lucrative business linked to large profits and run by powerful political and business interests, says Dr. Avinash Supe, Dean of civic-run King Edward Memorial (KEM) Hospital, Mumbai.

Private trusts that run new colleges have permission to charge huge fees and the regulatory bodies have turned a blind eye to these deficiencies and subversion of minimum standards, "passively caving in or actively succumbing to pecuniary temptations," he alleges.

The Medical Council of India (MCI) has been criticised for its failure in regulating these colleges. But the Central government too is unable to get involved in regulating exorbitant fees.

"We have no power to regulate at the Central level. There is a Supreme Court ruling that instructs appointing a state-level committee led by a retired High Court judge to fix fee structures. Any deviation from such a ruling should be checked by state authorities," says the Health Ministry's Arun Singhal, Additional Secretary, Medical Education.

The National Medical Commission has a provision for Government to decide the fees for 50 per cent of the seats in private and deemed medical colleges.

Medical Colleges

In India, a medical college is an educational institution that provides medical education. These institutions may vary from stand-alone colleges that train doctors to conglomerates that offer training related in all aspects of medical care. The term is synonymous with "medical school" as used in the US and some other countries.

Recognition

Indian law requires these institutions to be recognised by the Medical Council of India. The Indian government keeps an updated list of these approved medical colleges.

Admissions

Admissions to courses in medical colleges of India have been streamlined in the last few years. The whole admission process is under a major reform with ongoing court cases from parties against it. In general, admission was based on one of the following:

1 Marks obtained in the competitive examinations conducted at central level (NEET)
2 Marks obtained in the final examinations of Std. XII
3 Donation/Management based seats.

Similarly, for Postgraduate degrees and diplomas (residencies) the competitive examinations conducted at central (NEET) level forms the basis for admission or donation based seats. Specific institutions may also require a personal interview of the candidate, but this is more in cases of sub-specialty courses.

These donation-based seats have come under heavy criticism because this makes effectively India the only country that authorises, as official policy, the sale of medical seats by private medical colleges, implicitly accepting the principle that the ability to pay, and not merit, is what counts. These illegal capitation fees range from ₹50 lakhs to ₹1 crore for a MBBS seat. For any medical seat a student from general category should minimum have scored 50 percentiles in NEET UG to get seat in UG courses. But medical colleges in states like Kerala, require minimum marks/ranks in their respective competitive entrance exams even for the management seats.

In order to reduce stress of multiple examinations and ensuring minimum competence and importantly with the purpose to weed out corruption in medical education across the country NEET-UG and NEET-PG were first proposed in the Vision 2015 by Board of Governors (BOGs) appointed after by the Government of India after dissolution of MCI.

Undergraduate

NEET-UG (Undergraduate), for MBBS and BDS courses, was conducted in 2013 by the Central Board of Secondary Education (CBSE). NEET-UG replaced the All India Pre Medical Test (AIPMT) and all individual MBBS exams conducted by states or colleges themselves. However, many colleges and institutes took a stay order and conducted private examinations for admission to their MBBS and BDS courses. Nevertheless, many other reputed institutes such as the Armed Forces Medical College and Banaras Hindu University have opted to admit students on the basis of the NEET-UG. The first exam was held on 5 May 2013, and the results were announced on 5 June 2013. In India, there is a huge competition to qualify for an MBBS seat. In NEET-UG 2013, among the registered candidates, a total of 7,17,127 candidates were eligible to appear in the NEET-UG/2013, out of which 6,58,040 candidates appeared in the test and 3,66,317 candidates qualified the test for 31,000 seats. This makes a 4.71% appearing the exam to securing a seat success rate.

On 18 July 2013 the Indian Supreme Court struck down the NEET exam with a 2:1 decision. The Medical Council of India has appealed for a review in August 2013, in May 2016 the Supreme Court of India cancelled all medical exams and NEET(UG) and NEET(PG) becomes the only way to get admission in almost all medical colleges of India. From 2019 NEET Examinations are conducted by the National Testing Agency (NTA).

Postgraduate

Similarly, for Postgraduation courses (residencies), the NEET-PG is the single eligibility cum entrance examination for MD/MS and postgraduate diploma courses. This effectively replaced the existing AIPGMEE and similar state level exams for entry into postgraduate courses. The first NEET-PG was conducted by the National Board of Examinations from 23 November – 6 December 2012, which was referred to as the testing window (with 24th, 25th, 28 November and 2 December as non-testing days). The test was a computer-based test unlike the traditional paper and pen based test AIIMS had been conducting over years for admission to 50% all India quota of postgraduate courses in the country. In all, 90,377 candidates took the exam.

Foreign Nationals

Apart from non-resident Indian (NRI) and person of Indian origin (PIO) quotas in different government as well as private colleges, Government of India has also allocated a number of seats for students from developing countries where facilities for medical education are inadequate. The exact number and country-based allocation of these reserved seats may vary annually.

Students seeking admission to the reserved seats are required to apply through the Indian Missions abroad or through the diplomatic missions of the respective countries in India. The Indian Embassy or High Commission in a country will be able to provide more information on request. The requirement for an entrance is usually waived for such sponsored candidates.

It is important to note that foreign nationals wishing to take seats through NRI quota should still qualify through NEET (at least for all government colleges) and seats will be allotted on merit in that quota from all the NRI candidates eligible. The fee structure for NRI candidates is also different.

Courses Offered

MBBS Undergraduate Course

A medical college offers graduate degree, Bachelor of Medicine and Bachelor of Surgery (MBBS). Only institutions offering MBBS course in its curriculum are referred to as a Medical Colleges. The college may teach Postgraduate as well as Paramedical courses.

The MBBS course starts with the basic pre and para-clinical subjects such as biochemistry, physiology, anatomy, microbiology, pathology and pharmacology. The students simultaneously obtain hands-on training in the wards and out-patient departments, where they interact with real patients for five long years. The curriculum aims to inculcate standard protocols of history taking, examination, differential diagnosis and complete patient management. The student is taught to determine what investigations will be useful for a patient and what are the best treatment options. The curriculum also contains a thorough practical knowledge and practice of performing standard clinical procedures. The course also contains a 12-month-long internship, in which an intern is rotated across various specialties. Besides standard clinical care, one also gets a thorough experience of ward management, staff management and counselling skills.

The degree awarded is "Bachelor of Medicine and Bachelor of Surgery". The minimum requirements for the MBBS course are 50% marks in physics, chemistry, biology and English in the '10+2' examinations. For reserved category students, the requirement is 40%. MBBS admissions are not centralised. The admission requirements differ across universities. Generally, students who attain higher marks in the qualifying examinations and in the Medical Entrance examinations conducted by various agencies are accepted onto the MBBS course.

Entrance examinations are conducted by the following agencies

- AIIMS Entrance Exams – All India Institute of Medical Sciences
- NEET (National Eligibility cum Entrance Test) – National Testing Agency
- JIPMER Entrance Exams – Jawaharlal Institute of Post-graduate Medical Education and Research

Postgraduate Courses

All the major colleges also have Postgraduate Degree or Diploma courses in their programmes. The awards conferred are Doctor of Medicine (MD), Doctor of Philosophy (Ph.D Medical), Master of Surgery (MS), Master of Science (M.Sc. Medical), or Diplomate of National Board (DNB)). The MD/MS degrees are offered by the universities affiliated to the Medical Council of India and the DNB degree is awarded by the National Board of Examinations, an independent autonomous body under the Ministry of Health, India. They are available in different streams of medical science such as General Medicine, General Surgery, Orthopedics, Radiodiagnosis, Radiotherapy, ENT, Obstetrics and Gynaecology, Ophthalmology, Anesthesia, Pediatrics, Community Medicine, Pathology, Microbiology, Forensic Medicine, Pharmacology, Anatomy, Physiology, etc. Degree courses are of three years' duration while diploma courses are of two years' duration. Following postgraduation, students can opt for further super-specialisation in their area of interest by opting for courses called DM or DNB (Doctorate of Medicine), or MCh or DNB (Master of Chirurgery/ Surgery) again of three years' duration.

An MD or a DNB (general medicine or pediatrics) is the basic requirement for specialisation in Cardiology, Nephrology, Neonatology, Gastroenterology, Neurology except for Clinical Hematology (Pathology or general medicine), etc., while an MS or a DNB (general surgery, ENT or Orthopedic surgery) is the basic requirement for Neurosurgery, Urology, Cardio-thoracic and Vascular Surgery, Gastrointestinal Surgery, Pediatric Surgery, Plastic Surgery, etc.

Family medicine has now become an area of priority in India, and many teaching hospitals offer DNB (Family Medicine).

Postdoctoral fellowship courses in Neuro-radiology, Neuro or Cardiac anesthesiology, etc. are offered by select institutions.

Other Health Care Courses in India

They include

1 B.A.M.S., Bachelor of Ayurvedic Medicine and Surgery followed by M.D.
2 B.N.Y.S., Bachelor of Naturopathy and Yogic Sciences followed by M.D.
3 B.U.M.S., Bachelor of Unani Medine and Surgery followed by M.D.
4 B.S.M.S., Bachelor of Siddha Medicine and Surgery followed by M.D.
5 B.H.M.S., Bachelor of Homeopathic Medicine and Surgery followed by M.D.

Ayurveda, Yoga and Naturopathy, Unani, Siddha, Homeopathy are collectively called as AYUSH – Alternative medicine.

1 M.Sc Medical, Ph.D Medical.
2 B.Sc, M.Sc Nursing
3 B.Sc Medical Lab Technology
4 B.Pharm, M.Pharm. PharmD, Ph.D
5 B.P.T, M.P.T, Ph.D (Physiotherapy)
6 [B.D.S], M.D.S [(Dental Surgery)]
7 [B.O.T] [Occupational Therapy]
8 B.Sc [Speech Therapy]
9 B.Sc [Neurology]

Internship and Residency

After successful completion of the MBBS course, one has to compulsorily work in the hospital attached to the medical college or in any other approved hospital allowed in some medical colleges, for a period of one year. This posting is called the Compulsory Rotary Residential Internship or the House Surgeon in Kerala/Tamil Nadu. The student gets the degree only after satisfactory completion of the CRRI. An Intern (also called an Internee or a CRRI) is posted in all the clinical departments of the hospital on a rotation basis. This gives him or her the basic clinical and practical knowledge about all the disciplines of medicine and makes the medical graduate fit to work in the community as a General Physician. The schedules of an intern is usually extremely exhaustive. For example, one may have to work for the whole night and then have to start the next day duty only after about one or two hours. This may last till the afternoon. 24-hour sleepless duty at a stretch is not uncommon and sometimes the scheduled breaks are also not allowed by the superiors. He or she is also paid a monthly stipend for his work in the hospital which differs in different medical colleges on the basis of the management. The person is licensed to practise medicine only after completion of this internship. And only after finishing internship, one can receive his MBBS degree and can pursue postgraduate studies.

Postgraduate Specialisations

Subject	Degree	Diploma
Anaesthesia	MD/DNB	DA
Anatomy	MS/DNB/M.Sc(Medical)	Not Applicable
Biochemistry	MD/DNB/M.Sc (Medical)	Not Applicable
Community Medicine/PSM	MD/DNB	DCM/DPH
Dermatology	MD/DNB	DDVL/DVD
ENT	MS/DNB	DLO
Family Medicine	MD/DNB	Not applicable
Forensic Medicine	MS/DNB	DFM
General Medicine	MD/DNB	Not applicable
General Surgery	MS/DNB	Not applicable
Microbiology	MD/DNB/M.Sc(Medical)	Not applicable
Nuclear Medicine	MD/DNB	DRM
Orthopaedics	MS/DNB	D Ortho
Ophthalmology	MS/DNB	DO/DOMS
Obs. and Gynaecology	MS/DNB	DGO
Palliative Medicine	MD	NA
Pathology	MD/DNB	DCP

Subject	Degree	Diploma
Pharmacology	MD/DNB/M.Sc(Medical)	Not applicable
Physiology	MD/DNB/M.Sc(Medical)	Not applicable
Paediatrics	MD/DNB	DCH
Psychiatry	MD/DNB	DPM
Pulmonology	MD/DNB	DTCD
Radiodiagnosis	MD/DNB	DMRD
Radiotherapy	MD/DNB	DMRT
Tropical	MD	DTMH

Critical Shortcomings

Despite enabling improvements in crucial health indicators like child mortality rates, India's health care system fails to provide adequate medical services to large parts of the country's growing population, especially in rural regions. Symptomatic of the crisis are India' five low levels of public health care spending, amounting to only 0.9 per cent of GDP in 2016. While public hospitals offer free health services, these facilities are understaffed, poorly equipped, and located mainly in metropolitan areas. Most health services are therefore provided by private facilities, and 65 per cent of medical expenditures in India are paid out of pocket by patients. Millions of families are consequently plunged into catastrophic debt or forced to forgo critical medical treatment altogether.

One of the most pressing problems is India's severe shortage of medical doctors. According to the World Health Organisation, the country has only 7.8 registered medical doctors per 10,000 people, compared with 18 doctors per 10,000 people in China, 21 in Colombia, and 32 in France. What's more, not all registered doctors in India are actively practising, and many are poorly trained. Consider that the majority of allopathic (science-based) practitioners in the country — 57 per cent — lack a formal medical qualification.

New Licensing Requirements: The National Exit Test

The NMC bill introduces for the first time a nationwide licensing examination for medical doctors in India — the National Exit Test (NEXT) devised by the NMC. Administered at the end of the final year of the MBBS programme, the test will be required to obtain a licence to practise and become registered as a medical professional in state and national registers. The NEXT will come into effect three years after the enactment of the NMC bill. It will be a universal requirement for all physicians, including foreign-educated medical graduates, who currently sit for a separate test, the Foreign Medical Graduates Examination. Doctors who practise without being registered are subject to punishment of up to one year of jail time. Passing the NEXT will also be a requirement for admission into postgraduate programmes in medical specialties, replacing other entrance examinations currently in place.

The government expects that the uniform graduation examination will over time ensure a consistent quality of medical education nationwide. Present Union Health Minister Dr. Harsh Vardhan has explained that the NEXT will ensure that the new NMC "moves away from a system of repeated inspections of [institutions and] infrastructure and focuses on outcomes rather than processes." Addressing concerns that the NEXT might make it more difficult to obtain licensure and thereby exacerbate the shortage of physicians in India, he clarified that there will be no limits to the number of times medical graduates can retake the NEXT exam.

New Medical Curriculum

In 2019, the MCI rolled out a new competency-based medical curriculum to align medical education more closely with the "changing health needs of the country" and promote a more patient-centered approach. While the curriculum stresses the acquisition of global medical competencies, it also seeks to produce graduates who are able to effectively provide medical services to India's local communities. Changes include the introduction of a foundation module to impart basic language, communication, and computer skills, as well as a more extensive AETCOM (attitude, ethics, and communication) module to prepare students to communicate with patients. The curriculum is more integrated across different medical subjects and provides clinical exposure earlier than before — during the first year of the MBBS programme. The summative assessment of students in year-end examinations has been augmented with a more consistent and continual assessment of core competencies.

In the last three decades, there have been focused initiatives to mainstream traditional and alternative systems of medicine in health care services in India. The first full-fledged department of Indian Systems of Medicine and Homeopathy (ISM&H) was created under the Ministry of Health and Family Welfare, Government of India, in March 1995 to promote and regulate the practice of alternative systems of medicine in the country (Box 3). This department was, in November 2003, renamed as Department of Ayurveda, Yoga and Naturopathy, Unani, Siddha and Homeopathy (AYUSH). A fully independent Ministry of AYUSH was formed in November 2014. The Government of India also formulated the National Policy on Indian Systems of Medicine and Homeopathy.

Sustained efforts over the years have resulted in an increased availability of providers in alternative systems of medicine. By the end of March 2017, there were 3,943 hospitals and 27,698 dispensaries under AYUSH systems, under different administrative controls ranging from State and Union governments, local bodies and others (i.e. Central Government Health Services (CGHS); Railway, Coal and Labour Ministry and also run by research councils and national institutes). In March 2018, there were 773,668 already registered AYUSH practitioners, most of them being in Ayurveda followed by Homeopathy. There were 622 institutions offering undergraduate courses (annual intake of 40,151) and 201 institutes offering postgraduate courses (annual intake of 5,486) in AYUSH systems (Table 1).

The current National Health Policy of India has proposed functional linkage of AYUSH at all levels of health systems, including service delivery as well as work force. The policy proposal focuses on inclusion of Yoga at workplace, in schools and in the community as an important form of promoting health and wellness. The utilisation of AYUSH services ranges from 5-10 per cent of total health service utilisation with variations across Indian states (Government of India, 2014). In the year 2015-16, people in India spent around ₹63,000 crore on AYUSH health services (public and private sector put together), which amounts to nearly 12 per cent of total health expenditure of ₹528,484 crore in the country as reported in National Health Accounts (MOHFW, 2018).

Discussion and Way Forward

The current and predicted increasing burden of chronic and non-communicable diseases (NCDs) is often considered the most urgent reason for developing and strengthening collaboration between conventional and Traditional & Community Medicine health sectors. The study of state level burden of diseases in India has highlighted the emerging burden of NCDs, which mandates higher provision of preventive and promotive health services, along with curative and diagnostic services. Many T&CM (especially Ayurveda, Yoga and Naturopathy) largely focus on principles of wellness and health promotion. There is a vast infrastructure and plenty of providers in these systems and it is a great opportunity to tackle NCDs as well as other emerging health challenges in the country.

Table 3.1 Human Resource Availability and Production Capacity for Traditional and Alternative Systems of Medicine in India (March 2017)

Already Registered Practitioners		Undergraduate Courses		Post Graduate Courses	
		No. of Institutions	Annual Intake	No. of Institutions	Annual Intake
Ayurveda	428,884	338	21,387	135	4,122
Unani	49,566	49	2,705	11	127
Siddha	8,505	09	520	02	94
Naturopathy	2,242	25	1,630	03	45
Homeopathy	284,471	201	13,909	50	1,098
Total AYUSH	773,668	622	40,151	201	5,486

Source: National Health Profile of India, 2018.

The global evidence has pointed towards the need for task shifting (assigning some of the tasks done by allopathic doctors to other cadres of health care providers) in health systems.

Traditional/Indigenous/Alternative Systems of Medicine in India

Ayurveda

The Ayurvedic System of Medicine evolved nearly 5000 years ago (3000 B.C.). The word Ayurveda means 'Science of Life' and employs treatment modalities, such as purification, palliation, prescription of various diets, exercises and the avoidance of disease-causing factors. The Ayurvedic medicine, though practised for a wide range of health needs, is more commonly used for preventive and health and immunity boosting activities. Ayurveda is widely used in India and is more popular in Kerala, Himachal Pradesh, Gujarat, Karnataka, Madhya Pradesh, Rajasthan, Uttar Pradesh and Odisha.

Unani Medicine

Unani Medicine originated in the Arab world, though over a period of time it imbibed some concepts from other contemporary systems of medicines in Egypt, Syria, Iraq, Persia, India, China and other Middle East countries. Unani medicine treats a patient with diet, pharmacotherapy, exercise, massages and surgery. Unani Medicine was introduced in India around the 10th century AD and at present it is popular in the states of Andhra Pradesh, Kamataka, Tamil Nadu, Bihar, Madhya Pradesh, Maharashtra, Uttar Pradesh, Delhi and Rajasthan.

Homeopathy

The word 'Homeopathy' is derived from the Greek words, '*Homois*' meaning 'similar' and '*pathos*' means 'suffering'. It originated in Germany and was introduced in India around 1810-1839. Homeopathy is based on the law of healing — '*Similia SimilibusCurantur*' which means 'likes are cured by likes'. It uses highly individualised remedies selected to address specific symptoms or symptom profiles. It is practised in many countries and in India, where it is the second most popular system of medicine. Homeopathy is practised all over the country and is popular in Uttar Pradesh, Kerala, West Bengal, Odisha, Andhra Pradesh, Maharashtra, Punjab, Tamil Nadu, Bihar, Gujarat and North-Eastern States. In the recent years, the popularity of homeopathy has witnessed some decline.

Siddha

This system has originated in India and is amongst the oldest systems of medicine in the country. It takes into account the patient, his/her surroundings, age, sex, race, habitat, diet, appetite, physical condition, etc. to arrive at the diagnosis. Siddha System uses minerals, metals and alloys and drugs and inorganic compounds to treat the patients. Like most T&CM, this system is largely therapeutic in nature. Siddha literature is in Tamil and it is practised largely in Tamil-speaking part of India, Kerala and abroad.

Sowa-Rigpa

The word combination means the 'science of healing' and is considered one of the oldest living and well-documented medical traditions of the world. It originated from Tibet and is widely practised in India, Nepal, Bhutan, Mongolia and Russia. In India, this system is practised mainly in Sikkim, Arunachal Pradesh, Darjeeling (West Bengal), Dharamshala, Lahaul and Spiti (Himachal Pradesh), Ladakh and in parts of Delhi.

Table 3.2: Medical Colleges and Seats in India (2019)

Sl. No.	State	No. of Colleges	Seats
1	Andhra Pradesh	31	4850
2	A & N Islands	1	100
3	Assam	6	726
4	Arunachal Pradesh	1	50
5	Bihar	12	1300
6	Chandigarh	1	100
7	Chhattisgarh	9	1100
8	Delhi	8	1100
9	Goa	1	150
10	Gujarat	27	4500
11	Haryana	12	1600
12	Himachal Pradesh	7	750
13	Jammu & Kashmir	4	500
14	Jharkhand	3	350
15	Karnataka	57	8845
16	Kerala	34	4150
17	Madhya Pradesh	22	3100

Sl. No.	State	No. of Colleges	Seats
18	Maharashtra	51	7510
19	Manipur	2	200
20	Meghalaya	1	50
21	Mizoram	1	100
22	Odisha	11	1550
23	Puducherry	8	1200
24	Punjab	8	975
25	Rajasthan	21	3250
26	Sikkim	1	100
27	Tamil Nadu	49	6950
28	Telangana	27	4050
29	Tripura	2	200
30	Uttar Pradesh	48	6499
31	Uttarakhand	6	800
32	West Bengal	19	2850
33	AIIMS	9	807
34	JIPMER	1	200
	Total	501	70562

Yoga and Naturopathy

The concepts and practices of Yoga are reported to have originated in India. Yoga is now being adapted to correct lifestyle by cultivating a rational, positive and spiritual attitude towards all life situations. The role of Yoga techniques in the prevention and mitigation of diseases and promotion of health are being studied. Yoga is widely practised across India and has spread to many other parts of the world. The United Nations (UN) has designated 21st June as 'International Yoga Day'. Naturopathy or the naturopathic medicine is a drugless, non-invasive system of medicine imparted in treatments with natural elements based on the theories of vitality, toxemia and the self-healing capacity of the body, as well as the principles of healthy living. The common naturopathy modalities include counselling, diet and fasting therapy, mud therapy, hydrotherapy, massage therapy, acupressure, acupuncture, magnet therapy and yoga therapy.

4 Pharmacy Education

Pharmacy is the health profession that links the health sciences with the basic sciences; it is committed to ensuring the safe and effective use of medication. Pharmacists' professional roles and responsibilities have evolved historically from a focus on medication compounding and dispensing to extended pharmaceutical care services.

An increase in health demands, with a complex range of chronic medicines and poor adherence to prescribed medicines, has forced pharmacists to take a patient-centered approach. The paradigm shifts for pharmacy practice took turn in 1990, when Hepler and Strand introduced the term "pharmaceutical care". Over the last few decades, pharmacy organisations and academic training programmes around the world have promoted pharmaceutical care as a philosophy and standard of provision of care for patients. In essence, the pharmaceutical care concept has transformed the pharmacy profession to be more accountable in-patient care, especially to ensure that a patient achieves positive outcomes from drug therapy.

In many parts of the world, pharmacists have played a significant role in provision of pharmaceutical care services. In addition, it is also widely believed that pharmacists can make a great contribution to the provision of the primary health care, especially in developing countries. Their role varies in different parts of the world: some deal with the preparation and supply of medicines, while some focus on sharing pharmaceutical expertise with doctors, nurses and patients.

Pharmacy Profession in the International Context

WHO has contributed effectively towards encouraging and defending the role of pharmacists worldwide. Although all health care providers and the public are rationally involved in using drugs, WHO has recommended a special role for pharmacists, particularly in quality assurance and the safe and effective administration of drugs. The International Pharmaceutical Federation (FIP) and WHO developed the concept of "The seven-star pharmacist", which stated that a well-rounded pharmacist should be a compassionate care giver, decision maker, active communicator, lifelong learner and good manager; and should possess good leadership qualities and the ability to be a teacher and researcher. According to WHO, future pharmacists must possess specific knowledge, attitudes, skills and behaviours in support of their roles. Besides their pivotal role in public health, pharmacists can also act as advisors to physicians and nurses and contribute to policy decisions.

Evolution

India has been a country with a glorious past in various disciplines of knowledge which includes Pharmaceutical Sciences. The concept of Pharmacy evolved and was practised in ancient India. Ayurveda (Science of Life) and Siddha originated in India. The sources of drugs at that time were herbs and animals. Standardisation methods existed for converting herbs or animal extracts into potent medicines. Ayurveda then, was mostly practised by sages for the well-being of the mankind and was not exploited commercially. According to Hindu mythology, Lord Bramha was the first teacher who wrote about Ayurveda and defined it as the science of life. In 5000 B.C. Charaka and Sushrata spread the message of Ayurveda and educated people about its use and effectiveness.

The opening of a chemist shop in 1811 by Scotch in Bathgate, Kolkata was the start of pharmacy profession or practice in India. In 1870, a training programme for the chemists was started by the Madras Medical College which was later converted to a Diploma programme. Similarly, a one-year training course was also started for dispensing medicines through the Bengal Municipal Act. This laid the foundation of the pharmaceutical education in India. Since then the pharmaceutical education has undergone a radical change.

The year 1899 saw the dawn of modern Pharmaceutical Education. It was in this year that the modern pharmacy institutions commenced functioning for training of pharmacists in Madras (now Chennai). In 1928 the Medical Faculty of Bengal followed suit and started similar training programmes.

The systematic and well defined University education was initiated in 1932 when the Banaras Hindu University pioneered the pharmaceutical education under the guidance of Professor M. L. Shroff, the father of pharmaceutical education in India. Pharmaceutical Chemistry was introduced as a subject in the B.Sc Degree course in this year. A two year course of B.Sc Pharmaceutics was also introduced later. This further lead to the introduction of a three year Bachelor of Pharmacy (B.Pharmacy) course in 1937 at the Banaras Hindu University. The curriculum included Pharmacognosy, Pharmaceutical Chemistry and German and Pharmaceutical Economics. In 1940, a Master of Pharmacy (M.Pharm) research Degree was also introduced.

Subhadra Kumar Patni and Gorakh Prasad Shrivastava became the first Pharmacy graduates in 1940 and postgraduates in pharmacy in 1943 respectively. Similarly, Shevohari Lal became the first Ph.D holder in 1953 from the University of Patna. The list of first ten Pharmacy colleges and Universities offering degree programmes in Pharmacy are listed in Table 4.1.

The enactment of Pharmacy Act, 1948 founded the statutory regulation of pharmacy institutions in India. This was followed by the establishment of the Pharmacy Council of India by the Ministry of Health in 1949 and the first education regulation was framed in 1953.

These regulations were subsequently amended in 1972, 1981 and 1991 respectively. These bodies prescribed the minimum qualifications for being a registered pharmacist. The curriculum in those initial years included Pharmaceutical Chemistry and Analytical Chemistry and has subsequently evolved over a period of time to suit the requirements of various stakeholders, primarily the pharmaceutical manufacturing industry.

Table 4.1: List of First Ten Institutions Offering Courses in Pharmaceutical Sciences

S.No.	Name of University/College
1	Department of Pharmaceutical Engineering, Institute of Technology, Banaras Hindu University
2	University Institute of Pharmaceutical Sciences, Punjab University, Chandigarh
3	L. M. College of Pharmacy, Ahmedabad
4	Department of Pharmacy, Madras Medical College, Chennai
5	Birla Institute of Technology and Science, Pilani
6	College of Pharmaceutical Sciences, Andhra University, Vishakhapatnam
7	Department of Pharmaceutical Sciences, Dr. HarisinghGour University, Sagar
8	Department of Pharmaceutical Sciences, Nagpur University, Nagpur
9	Department of Pharmaceutical Sciences and Technology, Institute of Chemical Technology
10	Department of Pharmaceutical Technology, Jadhavpur University

Table 4.2 Status of Postgraduate Pharmacy Education in India

Year	Number of Institutes	Number of Faculty	Total Intake	Enrolment	Students Passed	Students Placed
2012-2013	822	6100	45947	20995	16421	8451
2013-2014	842	7596	51455	19997	16687	8831
2014-2015	845	8753	54540	18169	14631	7403
2015-2016	834	8413	50328	16145	–	5777
2016-2017	820	9678	46134	–	–	–

Due to the incremental growth of Pharmaceutical Industry in India, there has been a rapid expansion in the pharmaceutical education sector as well. The current status of postgraduate Pharmacy education in India is as summarised in Table 4.2.

Apart from the regular specialisations like Pharmaceutics, Quality assurance, etc. many sector specific specialisations have been introduced taking into consideration the requirements of the industry, which includes Pharmacoinformatics, Regulatory Affairs, Medical Devices, Pharmaceutical Management, to name a few.

India has been a hub of pharmaceutical manufacturing from the past three decades and is growing rapidly. It is expected to reach the 30 billion dollar mark by the year 2021.

It has thus impacted the content and the course curriculum of graduate and postgraduate courses in Pharmaceutical sciences across Public and Private Universities in India. It is unlike our counterparts in the United States and Europe, where it is mostly practice-based. The PCI through an amendment to the Pharmacy Act in 2008, paved the way for the Pharm.D. (Doctor of Pharmacy) course in India. The Pharm.D course focuses on Pharmacy Practice and emphasises the role of a pharmacist as one of the major stakeholders in the health care delivery infrastructure. JSS College of Pharmacy, Mysore was one of the first to start the Pharm.D course. According to PCI, there are 165 colleges offering 4950 seats for the Pharm.D course in the year 2016- 2017. The current status of Pharm.D course in India is summarised in Table 4.3.

Premier Institutes offering Post Graduate Courses in Pharmaceutical Sciences

With a view to create institutes of higher learning with world class infrastructure and delivering affordable education to masses in the field of Pharmaceutical Education, the Ministry of Chemicals and Fertilizers, Government of India established seven premier institutions by the

Table 4.3 Number of Colleges Conducting Pharm.D Course (State wise)

State	Number of Colleges	Number of Seats
Andhra Pradesh & Telangana	57	1710
Gujarat	06	180
Haryana	01	30
Karnataka	43	1290
Kerala	18	540
Madhya Pradesh	02	60
Maharashtra	07	210
Punjab	03	90
Rajasthan	01	30
Tamil Nadu	24	720
Uttar Pradesh	02	60
Uttarakhand	01	30

name National Institute of Pharmaceutical Education and Research (NIPER) offering various postgraduate courses in Pharmaceutical sciences since 1998. The first NIPER was set up at SAS Nagar, Mohali, Punjab followed by six more in the year 2007. The list of these institutions of national importance along with their year of establishment is given in Table 4.4. Four more NIPERs were announced in the year 2015 and will commence operations soon.

Table 4.4 List of NIPERS

S.No.	Name of the Institute
1	NIPER Mohali
2	NIPER Ahmedabad
3	NIPER Hajipur
4	NIPER Kolkata
5	NIPER Hyderabad
6	NIPER Guwahati
7	NIPER Rai Bareli
8	NIPER Nagpur
9	NIPER Rajasthan
10	NIPER Chhattisgarh
11	NIPER Tamil Nadu

NIPERs offer a two-year M.S. degree in fourteen disciplines including Medicinal Chemistry, Pharmacology and Toxicology, Pharmaceutical Analysis, Clinical Research, Natural Products, Pharmaceutical Analysis, Pharmacy Practice, Biotechnology, Pharmacoinformatics, Medical Devices, Pharmaceutics, Quality Assurance, Regulatory Toxicology, Traditional Medicine. NIPER Mohali also offers a Master's Programme in Pharmaceutical Management. Admissions to NIPER's are held in June-July on the basis of the score of a National Level Entrance test called as the NIPER Joint Entrance Test, whereas admissions to M.Pharm courses of Universities are done on the basis of the student's score in Graduate Pharmacy Aptitude Test (GPAT) conducted by the AICTE or a Common Entrance Tests (CET) conducted by the respective states.

Critical Evaluation of Pharmacy Education

Private unaided affiliated institutions offering postgraduate education in pharmaceutical sciences outnumber the government or aided institutions in India. With the liberalisation of the education policy, many private universities are being set up and most of them offer graduate and post graduate education in pharmaceutical sciences, thus making pharmaceutical education sector as one of the potential areas of employment.

It is beyond doubt that pharmaceutical education has made speedy expansion and progress in its various forms. But how far have we succeeded in accomplishing our objective or are we still lagging behind is a debatable issue. The curriculum is still far from establishing collaborations with the Industry and its requirements especially given the constraints in which most of the institutions operate.

Technology needs to be used adequately so that trained pharmacists could rise to the occasion for playing an important role in the health care sector nationally and globally. We have failed greatly in this regard since the education sector in general is where the concept of using technology to increase productivity remains a not-so-important proposition.

Pharmaceutical education should come out of the traditional mode and needs to gear up to fulfill the present-day requirements of the industry and society in general. Despite efforts being taken by various regulatory bodies, the pharmaceutical industry has always voiced for not being able to get readily employable students who could turn productive in a short span of time for them. Moreover, the way in which the Indian health care industry is progressing, we would see an increased demand for practising pharmacists, who would assist the physicians and patients.

The Pharmaceutical education in India needs to focus, not only on developing theoretical and technical knowledge but should to a large extent focus on actual technical skills and acumen required by the Industry, for making students employable.

As far as practice-based education is concerned, technical knowledge, establishing and maintaining good relationships with patients and physicians would be of prime importance. Unfortunately, it is awfully lacking today. It also requires adequate attention towards clinical efforts in the hospital and the involvement of Pharmacists as an integral part of the health care delivery system.

The pharmaceutical education sector needs a paradigm change to meet the ever-growing and ever-changing requirements of the pharmaceutical industry. Sincere efforts by all the stakeholders are required to raise the level of pharmaceutical education and to produce graduates and post-graduates who are employable and productive from day one. Active participation of the industry in training the students and teachers is highly desirable. Revision of curriculum at timely intervals with active inputs from the industry is required to achieve this Herculean task. Moreover, intervention by the Government and Regulatory bodies is essential to place pharmacists in an appropriate role and position to strengthen the health care delivery systems in India.

Pharmacy Council of India (PCI)

Pharmacy courses in India are among the most popular courses. The study of pharmacy involves health sciences and chemical sciences and pharmacists are pharmaceutical experts and primary health professionals. Pharmacy education and profession in India is regulated by the Pharmacy Council of India (PCI). It is a statuary body formed under the provisions of Pharmacy Act, 1948.

Responsibilities of PCI

1. regulates the practice of pharmacy in India.
2. prescribes standards required for pharmacist to practise in India.
3. frames educational regulations for institutions providing pharmacy education.
4. approves the course of study and examination for pharmacists.
5. maintains a central register of pharmacists.
6. ensures uniform standard of pharmacy education in the country.

Pharmacy Courses

D.Pharm

Diploma in Pharmacy is popularly known as D.Pharm in India. It is a two year-undergraduate course offered by pharmacy colleges. D.Pharm is the minimum qualification required to become a registered pharmacist in India. D.Pharm course does not provide specialised education; the basic concepts of pharmaceutical science is taught. A candidate who wishes to pursue this course is required to pass the senior secondary examination with physics, chemistry and biology or mathematics as optional subjects.

B.Pharm

B.Pharm is four-year undergraduate degree which enables candidates to practise as professional pharmacists. The courses cover health care and biochemical science. The basic eligibility for studying for B.Pharm is a pass in the Senior Secondary Examination with 50 per cent marks. The candidate should have studied physics, chemistry and mathematics. In some states it is necessary to take the entrance test to get a place.

B.Pharm Entrance Exams

Objective type questions are asked in exam. Mostly the duration of the test is one hour and 30 minutes and the test covers physics, chemistry, biology and mathematics at the higher secondary level.

Major B.Pharm entrance exams are:

1. Banaras Hindu University BAMS/B.Pharmacy Entrance Test
2. B.Sc Pharma Entrance Exam, Maharshi Dayanand University
3. VELS University Entrance Examination
4. Maharashtra B.Pharm Common Entrance Test
5. Himachal Pradesh University Shimla B.Pharma Entrance Test
6. B.Sc Pharma Common Entrance Exam, Kerala
7. B.Sc Pharma Entrance Exam in Punjab
8. State Entrance Examination, Uttar Pradesh
9. Rajasthan Pre Entrance Test for Pharmacy
10. B.Sc Pharma Entrance Exam, Bareilly.

M.Pharm

Master of Pharmacy (M.Pharm) is a postgraduate programme in India. Candidates who wish to do M.Pharm are required to gain B.Pharm first. The two-year course lays emphasis on research and specialisation in the field of pharmacy. There are several colleges in India offering M.Pharm in various specialties like pharmacology, pharmaceutics, pharmacognosy and pharmaceutical biotechnology.

M.Pharm Entrance Exams

Objective type questions are asked in the entrance test and duration of the test is usually two hours. The entrance test is based on the curriculum for undergraduate pharmacy course. The important tests are listed below:

1. The National Institute of Pharmaceutical Education and Research (NIPER) JEE Entrance Test
2. Kerala CEE Entrance exam for M.Pharm
3. Bharath Vidyapeeth University entrance test for pharmacy courses
4. Manipal university entrance test for M.Pharm.

Pharm.D

Pharm.D is a pre-Ph.D, postgraduate programme introduced in India to improve clinical pharmacy services. The entry requirement for this six-year programme is senior secondary education with mathematics and science as optional subjects. The course involves five years of academic activity and one year of internship.

Entrance exam

Most of the institutes offer admission to Pharm.D course on the basis of an entrance test held by the concerned University/College/Autonomous Institution. Some of the popular entrance tests for Pharm.D course are listed below:

1. Amrita Viswavidyapeeth Pharm-D entrance examination
2. Manipal University Online Entrance Test and Engineering
3. All India Entrance Test for Pharm-D
4. Agriculture and Medical Common Entrance Test (EAMCET)

Ph.D in Pharmacy

Candidates who have done M.Pharm can do Ph.D in pharmacy. Admission is on the basis of educational background, profile and interview. Some colleges offering Ph.D in India;

1. Manipal University Pharmacy College
2. Delhi Institute of Pharmaceutical Science and Research.
3. Culcutta Institute of Pharmaceutical Technology and Allied Sciences
4. Birla Institute of Technology, Ranchi
5. Sri Ramachandra University, Chennai

Qualitative and Quantitative Paucity of Talent

Pharmacy education has a major role to play in the progress of the pharma sector. Yet, in India, it is entangled in several issues. One of the major issues is the implementation of the right courses as academic programmes are structurally not organised to meet industry expectations. This has resulted in a large number of vacancies in the organised sector along with a high rate of unemployment among the skilled categories.

Understanding the criticality of the issue, Express Pharma spoke to industry experts to find out how these issues can be resolved.

The topic was also addressed at the recently held FDD Conclave organised by Express Pharma. An expert panel discussed the various challenges faced by the sector due to qualitative and quantitative paucity of talent and the role of academic institutions in creating better talent in terms of quality and quantity.

1. Right talent pool

In the recent years, we have seen a lot of pharmacy colleges mushrooming across the country, especially in rural India. However, a constant lament is that students from many from these institutes lack exposure due to an outmoded curriculum changes and various other factors. So, how can we ensure that we create the right talent pool which is industry-ready?

"It is not that we don't have the right talent pool but the main problem is lack of exposure. Students belonging to rural areas have never seen a pharmacy college in their life and upgrading the talent pool remains a big challenge."

Pointing out the reasons for lack of skill-based training at the academic level, Dr Arun Garg, Dean, SMAS KR Mangalam University, highlights, "The quality of education in Pharmacy Council of India (PCI) approved diploma colleges is a concern because most of the institutes provide education through distance mode/non-attending mode. This prevents student from learning necessary practical skills expected by the community/hospital/industry. Hands-on training in any course is the necessary gap that needs to be urgently bridged so a student can understand the value and essence of the programme he/she is undertaking. It also helps a candidate analyse his/her role to play as a pharmacist in the society."

2. Upgrading the syllabus

The current syllabus followed in pharmacy colleges, as per the industry experts, is outdated. This, in turn, has taken a toll on nurturing the right talent. With advancements in pharma technology, students along with industry stakeholders should remain updated on the current scenario.

The outdated pharmacy syllabus is affecting industrial growth and there has been a large hue and cry to revise the syllabus; however, nothing much has happened on this front. "The elements of the course have become outdated and provide no or little interaction with the status and growth of the pharma industry. It becomes necessary to follow the rapid and continuous changes in pharma industry, which makes academia-industry interaction a necessity. The curriculum should be revamped to have more case study or actual practical-based syllabus. This would require inputs from the industry during the point of framing of syllabus. Practicals need to be designed based on problems encountered by the industry during the product development process, right from pre-formulation stage to regulatory filing."

There is a complete disconnect between theoretical education and its application in practice. There is an urgent need to bridge the gap. A few points need to be considered to bridge the gap.

These include:

- How much theory is connected to industrial practice or pharmacy practice or to other requirements at the place of work?
- In what way is the 'theory' connected with 'practical' work?
- What is the real outcome of theoretical training? Can it not be translated into some tangible outcomes?
- Which specific skills have you been able to impart through the practicals attached to the theory course included in the syllabus?
- What are the specific applications or outcomes?
- How do you connect the basic concepts and the skills imparted? What is their actual application in industry/market/workplace, etc?

3. Innovation drives drug delivery

Innovation in drug delivery method is the future of Indian pharma industry. Pharmacy course structure in India mainly consists of two facets of profession: patient (pharmacy practice) and product (industrial pharmacy) oriented pharmacy in different proportions together. However, this approach did not witness much success as the course structure for practising pharmacy is not relevant to the requirements of an industry, and vice-versa.

Even after having more than 700 pharmacy colleges which offer M.Pharm every year and 15000 students passing out from these colleges looking for a career in R&D have suffered at the behest of quantity. "On one hand, the number of colleges imparting B.Pharm and M.Pharm have mushroomed to an exorbitant number over the last 10 years, while on the other hand the quality of students has suffered at the behest of quantity. This has completely skewed the demand-supply ratio as there is no dearth of students who major in pharmaceutics. Besides this, the research and development work in industry may not match with what is done in the academics. For example, research in academics is mainly happening in areas like nanotechnology while that is not so in the industry."

As Dr. N. Udupa, Professor and Research Director (Health Sciences), Manipal Academy of Higher Education, suggests, "Pharma companies willing to develop their drug delivery research centres should come forward to collaborate with highly ranked pharma institutions to train talented students and in collaboration should conduct and explore joint research projects in drug delivery. They should bring out novel patents and technology transfer should take place in right time as per future needs."

4. Volume to value

To move from volume to value, we need to find an answer to the questions whether we have skilled talent available within the industry. We also need to create an ecosystem which appreciates and acknowledges quality and excellence. Our experts have diverse views on achieving this objective.

Government should work together in creating an ecosystem which encourages innovation right from the academic level.

"Volume to value is a great mission. If we publish a successful story and give respect to contributors with academy-industry collaboration, everybody will think of the output with quality. We have to create certain standards to measure the effectiveness of such associations, then only we can progress towards value addition. This will encourage many colleges and industries to go for collaboration."

"The industry can make their own assessments and identify talented students/staff from the academic institutions from time to time and work on short and long-term projects. Students and staff can be given incentives in the form of some rewards or scholarships. This will also initiate specific and relevant projects that are applicative and translational in nature."

5. Government's initiatives

Fortunately, recognising the need for an overhaul in the education system and build a talent pool, the government too is introducing measures to meet this goal. For instance, the Life Sciences Sector Skill Development Council (LSSSDC), has been established by and for the life sciences sector in India, to address the skill gaps across functional areas and levels in the sector, by helping to generate a sustained stream of high quality skilled individuals.

The industry feels that there is a lot more that the government can do to promote and improve education and skill building for the pharmacy sector in the country. "The government needs to draw out priorities for the next three to five years and align with the industry with specific objectives relevant to the country and according to the context of the new environment. Funding provided by government agencies can be directed on such projects of national importance in order to make a match with the industry. All such projects should have commercial value so that the industry is attracted to pursue them."

Going Forward

Pharmacy education in India needs to be at par with global standards, where students armed with all required expertise can grow up the career ladder. This can be achieved only if industry and academia come on a single platform for a better tomorrow.

5 Nursing Education

...Nursing yesterday was guiding
...Nursing today is inspiring
...Nursing tomorrow will be challenging.

Nurses are two-thirds of health workforce in India. Their central roles in healthcare delivery in terms of promotion, prevention, treatment, care and rehabilitation are highly significant. Their contributions towards achieving UN millennium development goals (MDG) and sustainable development goals (SDG) are very crucial but not sufficient enough particularly in developing countries like India to create major impact on health outcomes. Achieving universal coverage, increasing health financing, recruitment, training and retention of health workforce are two important goals that have direct relevance to India. Nursing today has witnessed several changes, successes and challenges through a lot of stride and movement. Nurses have widened the scope of their work. However, while the roles and responsibilities have multiplied, there are still concerns with regard to development of nursing workforce selection and recruitment, placement as per specialisation, pre service, in-service training and human resource (HR) issues for their career growth.

Trends in Development

Nursing had originated independently and existed for many centuries without contact with modern medicine. Family members at home met the nursing needs of the sick persons. Evolution of medicine, surgery and public health into complicated technical area requiring many procedures by persons specially trained and having understanding of scientific principles brought two professions closer and together.

British Period

After the Mughal period, the nursing in India was hindered due to various reasons like low status of women, system of Parda among Muslims, caste system among Hindus, illiteracy, political unrest and nursing being looked upon as servants work. During the 16th century nursing development in India took three dimensions: 1) Military nursing 2) Civilian nursing 3) Miscellaneous nursing. On February 21, 1888, 10 fully qualified nurses from Florence Nightingale arrived in Bombay to lead nursing in India. This paved the way to develop one of the best nursing in the world. In 1894 regular system of training for men for hospital work started. Some men volunteerily did the course and applied for nursing certificate. This laid the foundation to existing system of training. In 1927 Indian military nursing services formed with 12 matrons, 18 sisters, and 25 nurses. They were made responsible for supervision, institution and training of nursing services for entire Indian Hospital Corps. Second World War expanded nursing service. 3-year training started in Military hospitals. After Second World War, government started short courses of intensive training in 1942 which led to the Auxiliary Nursing Services. From 1888 to 1893 experts drew upon curriculum for training. In 1926 Midwives Registration Act formed for the purpose of better training of midwives. In 1908 Trained Nurses Association of India (TNAI) was formed. In 1910 TNAI published journal. In 1912 TNAI affiliated to International Nursing Council as 8th Association in the world.

Post-Independence Period

Many committees and commissions were established and many reforms were initiated in nursing field. INC was established and many changes took place. Today Nursing Council is a statutory body that regulates nursing education in the country through prescription, inspection, examination, certification and maintaining standard in nursing field.

Recommendations of Various Committees Pertaining to Nursing Education

The recommendations given by committees and commissions provided guidelines for improvement and growth of nursing education.

1. Health survey and development committee (Bhore committee 1946)
    - Establishment of nursing college
    - Creation of an all India nursing council

2. Shetty committee 1954
   - Improvement in conditions of training of nurses
   - Minimum requirement for admission to be in accordance with regulation of the INC
3. Health survey and planning committee (Muralidhar committee 1959-61)
   - Three grades of nurses: the basic nurses (4 years), auxiliary nurse midwife (2 years) and nurses with a degree qualification
   - For GNM, minimum entrance qualification matriculation
   - For degree course, passed higher secondary or pre university
   - Medium of instruction preferably English in General nursing
   - Degree course should be taught only in English
4. Mukherjee Committee 1966
   - Training of nurses and ANM's required for family planning
5. Kartar Singh committee 1972-73
   - Multiple purpose health worker scheme
   - Setting up of training division of the Ministry of Health and Family Welfare
6. Sarojini Varadappan Committee 1990 (A high power committee on nursing and nursing profession)
   - Two levels of nursing personnel
   - Post basic B.Sc nursing degree to continue
   - Masters in nursing programme to be increased and strengthened
   - Doctorate in nursing programme to be started in selected universities
   - Continuing education and staff development for nurses
7. Working Group on Nursing Education and Manpower 1991
   - By 2020 the GNM program to be phased out
   - Curriculum of B.Sc nursing to be modified
   - Staffing norm should be as per INC
   - There should be deliberate plan for preparation of teachers M.Sc/M.Phil and Ph.D degrees improvement in functioning of INC
   - Importance of continuing education for nurses.

Summary of Evolution

We can summarise the history of Nursing Education in India as follows:

1871 School of nursing started in general hospital Madras

1886 School of nursing in a full-fledged form was started in JJ hospital, Bombay

1892 Many hospitals in Bombay started nursing associations which were intended to provide additional facilities for the training of local nurses
1908 TNAI was established
1909 Bombay Presidency nursing association was formed
1910 United board of examination for nurses was organised
1913 South India board was organised
1926 First nurses registration act passed in Madras
1935 Madras and Bombay nursing councils were established
1942 ANM programme started
1943 School of nursing at RAK college, New Delhi
1943 Diploma programme in nursing administration started in New Delhi
1946 4-year B.Sc nursing programme started in RAK college and CMC Vellore
1947 INC Act was passed
1949 INC was established
1959 M.Sc nursing started at RAK college
1963 Post basic B.Sc programme started in various institutions
1968 M.Sc nursing in CMC Vellore
1972 Basic degree programme started in Kerala
1985 M.Sc nursing started in CMC Ludhiana
1985 IGNOU established
1986 Curriculum change for GNM programme from 31/2 years to 3 years
1986 M.Phil programme started in RAK, New Delhi
1987 Separate directorate of nursing was created in Karnataka state
1988 M.Sc Nursing in NIMHANS
1992 Ph.D programme started in RAK College, New Delhi
1992 Post basic programme started under IGNOU
1994 M.Sc nursing started at Mahe, Manipal
1994 Basic B.Sc programme under School of Medical Education in Mahatma Gandhi University, Kottayam
1996 M.Phil and Ph.DMahe, Manipal
2001 Ph.D at NIMHANS.

Nursing Education

1. Auxiliary Nurse Midwifery (ANM)

ANM is medical nursing course that focuses on the care of individual, families and communities. The duration of the course ranges from 1 to 3 years depending on the institution. The minimum education requirement for doing this course is Senior Secondary Education with 45% marks. At the end of the course, the candidates can work as multiple health workers. The focus is on community health nursing. In some states, this course is offered after 10th class as part of vocational training.

2. General Nursing and Midwifery (GNM)

General nursing and midwifery course is conducted in several institutions across the country. The focus of general nursing is the care of the sick in hospitals. Schools of nursing are attached to teaching hospitals. The candidates need to have passed the senior secondary examinations. Both science and arts students are eligible for study. The duration is three years.

3. Graduate Nursing Program (B.Sc Nursing)

There are two types of graduate nursing education in India. The 4-year basic course for fresh entrants and the post-basic courses for those who have already done the GNM course.

1. B.Sc Nursing 4-years

The entry qualification is Senior Higher Secondary Education in biological sciences, physics and chemistry. The course focuses on grooming professional nurses. The course provides balanced professional and general education and enables students to become professional nurses. The course prepares nurses to work at bedside and take up leadership roles and public health nursing.

2. Post-Basic B.Sc Nursing

This two year nursing programme is for those who have already done GNM. The course provides opportunity for higher education to practising nurses. The duration of the course is two years.

4. Postgraduate Degree in Nursing

M.Sc in Nursing is offered in many universities. The entry requirements is B.Sc Nursing with two years' experience. Besides, most of the universities conduct entrance test. The course trains nurses to be clinical and community health nursing specialists. At this level the students are taught to carry out research in nursing.

5. M.Phil in Nursing

RAK college started M.Phil in Nursing in 1980. Now several universities offer M.Phil programme. This one year programme provides basic training required for research in undertaking doctoral work.

6. Ph.D in Nursing

The Ph.D programme started in India in 1992. A candidate wishing to pursue Ph.D needs to have gained an M.Phil degree and the second class Masters degree. The duration is three years.

Nursing Speciality and Area of Practice

There was a time professional nurse had very little choice of service because nursing was centred in the hospital on bedside nursing. Career opportunities are more varied now for a number of reasons. Career options include:

- A staff nurse provides direct patient care to one patient or a group of patients. Assists ward management and supervision. Directly responsible to the ward supervisor.
- Ward sister or nursing supervisor, responsible to the nursing superintendent for the nursing care management of a body or unit. Takes full charge of the ward. Assigns work to nursing and non-nursing personnel working in the ward. Responsible for safety and comfort of patients in the ward. Provides teaching sessions if it is a teaching hospital.
- Department supervisor/assistant nursing superintendent responsible to the nursing superintendent and deputy nursing superintendent for the nursing care and management of more than one ward or unit, for example, the surgical department or outpatient department.
- Deputy nursing superintendent responsible to the nursing superintendent and assists in the nursing administration of the hospital.
- Nursing superintendent responsible to the medical superintendent for safe and efficient management of hospital nursing services.
- A Director of Nursing is responsible for both nursing service and nursing education within a teaching hospital.
- Community Health Nurse (CHN) services focus on reproductive child health programmes.
- Teaching in nursing. The functions and responsibilities of the nursing instructor include planning, teaching and supervising the learning experiences for students. Positions in nursing education include Clinical Instructor, Tutor, Senior Tutor, Lecturer and Associate Professor, Reader in nursing and Professor in nursing.
- Industrial nurses provide first aid, care during illness, health education about industrial hazards and prevention of accidents.

- The Military Nursing Service became part of Indian Army, and nurses became commissioned officers who earned ranks from lieutenant to major general.
- Nursing service abroad, salaries and professional opportunities have led to increase in nursing service abroad.
- Nursing services administrative positions. At the state level, the Deputy Director of Nursing at the state health directorate. The highest administrative position on a national level is the Nursing Advisor to the Government of India.
- Nursing informatics is also an area of practice for nurses in India.
- Independent Nurse Midwife Practitioner pilot project completed successfully, four candidates are successfully trained.

Challenges in Nursing Education in India

Dr. Padmaraj Meera in the Commonwealth Nurses Conference held at London in 2012 highlighted the following challenges in Nursing Education in India:

1. Faculty development and faculty vacancies of critical challenges
    - to meet the need of maintaining nurse population ratio, more manpower generation is needed
    - quality of the product has to be preserved
    - educators need the training to enable them to incorporate evidence-based practice
    - upgraded competencies in health profession education
    - research skills
    - improved incentives and rewards is the major issue
    - it is a tough challenge for the regulatory bodies.
2. Lack of Support for continuing nursing education
    - lack of educational development and access, quality and safety issues leading to poor performance
    - lifelong learning should be emphasised with information technology
    - periodic knowledge and skill update be given
    - this aspect needs great attention and effort from government and professional bodies.
3. Minimise theory practice gap and improving clinical skills
    - theory practice gap is so wide in India due to various reasons
    - learnt theory to practice in clinical setting is minimal
    - providing good clinical exposure
    - collaboration between nursing education and service.

4. Curtail unethical practice existing in the field of Nursing Education
   - many unethical practices exist in the country
   - some of the institutions enroll as regular candidates on the roll but they are permitted to attend the final exams
   - Indian Nursing Council instructed to curtail unethical practices.
5. The action taken by Indian Nursing Council to meet the lacunae and challenges
   - development of nursing education at National level by involving the nursing professional organisation and stakeholders
   - to review nursing curriculum
   - development and strengthening continuing education
   - strengthen nursing research
   - upgradation of nursing education to B.Sc, M.Sc and Ph.D levels
   - qualifications of nurse educators to be strengthened
   - to empower the nurses in policy decisions
   - conformity of nursing education standard with Quality Assurance System
   - stern action against unethical practices.

Conclusion

Nursing practice in the 21st century faces a number of challenges around the globe in general, and particularly in India. Develop from knowledge base and range of competencies capable of supporting new skills and knowledge as they emerge. One needs to be a self directed learner throughout the working lifetime to meet the challenges, relevance, and quality care to the clients.

Education is human conversation with life. This implies about the needs, problems, pain, joys, dreams and hopes of people and the world a huge classroom where life is a continuous process of education.

6 Business Management Education

Management education has a vital role to play in today's business environment, where everything changes so fast that it makes it difficult for organisations to survive the growing competition. This has led to the need for business schools in developing nations to impart relevant education, which reflects the changes in the society.

Management education in recent times has received enormous attention and gaining importance in India. The economic liberalisation, globalisation, industrialisation and privatisation over the past decades are a few of the important reasons for gaining importance of management education. The challenges in management education are manifold in terms of institution building, enhancing the educational quality, covering global perspectives, developing ethical standards, seeking industrial collaborations and developing new perspectives in the management thought.

Management education adds value to the existing qualifications. It enhances managerial and leadership skills by sharing of ideas, insights through healthy, meaningful and case study discussions. Apart from providing requisite skills and abilities to get going smoothly in the corporate world, it provides an opportunity to network with others and promises cross-cultural diversity. It helps in equipping the executives with competencies and capabilities to take on the corporate challenges with confidence.

Time Line

Business Management Education has a long history in India, dating back to the 19th century. Early Business Schools were focused on the commercial side of business, aiming to fulfill the needs of the then foreign government.

- India's first B School i.e., Commercial School of Pacchiappa Charities was set up in 1886 in the southern city of Madras (now Chennai).
- The first level Business School was founded in 1913, in Mumbai i.e., Sydenham College.
- The Indian Institute of Social Science founded in the year 1948 as India's first management programme with an intention to train manpower to create and spread the knowledge, required for managing industrial enterprises in India.
- IIM-Calcutta established in collaboration with the Sloan School of Management (MIT) for faculty and pedagogy development in the year 1961, with an intention to focus on quantitative and operational aspects of management.
- IIM-Ahmedabad was founded in 1962, pioneering the case method of teaching in India.
- The mission of IIMs was to professionalise Indian Management education through teaching, research, training, institution-building and consulting with the support of expertise developed by the pioneering IIMs.
- Two more IIMs were founded in Bengaluru (Karnataka) and Lucknow (U.P.) in 1973.
- In late 1990's, two more IIMs were setup, one at Kozhikode (Kerala) and the other at Indore (M.P.).

The early 1990s showed a boom of founding new management schools, most of them are in private sector. Few B-Schools got established in collaboration with some western universities.

Management education in India is in the phase of change. The two current developments sweeping India, namely liberalisation and globalisation, have had a considerable impact on management education. Today, there are several B Schools in the country, spread over in different states of India.

Present Structure

The present structure, divided into six categories, is as follows:

1 Indian Institutes of Management (HMS) set up by Government of India.
2 University Departments of Management studies, distance, correspondence and part time courses as well.

3 Colleges and institutes affiliated to universities.
4 Private or government institutes approved by All India Council for Technical Education (AICTE).
5 Private institutes or colleges not affiliated to any universities and not approved by AICTE.
6 Private colleges or institutes offering MBA courses in India in collaboration with foreign universities, where degree and diploma certificates are awarded by the foreign universities.

Courses

Since inception, different courses in management education are developed like Certificate, Diploma, Bachelor Degree, PG Diploma, Master Degree, etc. In addition to this Bachelor of Business Administration (BBA), Bachelor of Business Studies (BBS) and Bachelor of Business Management (BBM) are the courses introduced at graduation level. Post Graduate Diploma in Business Management (PGDBM). Post Graduate Diploma in Management (PGDM), PGDDRM and PGDHEM are few prominent diploma courses. Master of Business Management (MBM) and Master of Business Administration (MBA), Master of International Business (MIB), Master of Management Programme (MMP), Master of Performance Management (MPM), Master of Personnal Management (MPM), Master of Business Studies (MBS) are the courses at master level given through entrance exams MAT (Management Aptitude Test), GMAT (Graduate Management Aptitude Test), CET (Common Admission Test), ATMA, EMAT, XAT, CEMAT, OPENMAT, IIFT (IIFT entrance test for IIFT, BIMTECH) etc., are conducted in India.

Master of Business Administration (MBA) attracts from the wide range of academic disciplines. The core courses in the MBA programme are designed to introduce students to the various areas of business, such as accounting, finance, marketing, human resources, operations management, etc., Students in MBA programmes have options of taking general business courses throughout the programme or can select specialisation areas. Accreditation bodies exist specifically for MBA programmes to ensure consistency and quality of graduate business education.

Master of Business Administration (MBA) courses are of two years and divided into four semesters, and subjects taught in all the four semesters relates to management education like Accounting for business Decisions, Economic Analysis for Business Decisions, Legal Aspects of Business, Business Research Methods, Organisational Behaviour, Basics of Marketing, Marketing Management, Financial Management,

Human Resource Management, Management Information Systems, Strategic Management, Enterprise Performance Management, Start-up and New Venture Management, Information Technology, Operations Management, Human Resource Management, International Business Management, Supply Chain Management, Rural and Agri-business Management, Managing for Sustainability, subject core courses in Marketing and Finance.

Overseeing Agencies

Department of Higher Education, MHRD: The Ministry of Human Resource Development has two departments namely Department of School Education and Literacy and the Department of Higher Education. The latter department works for the planned development of higher education through 100 autonomous bodies including the UGC, AICTE, IIMs, IITs, etc.

All India Council for Technical Education (AICTE): The All India Council for Technical Education (AICTE) was set up in November 1945 as a national level Apex Advisory Body to conduct survey on the facilities on technical education and to promote development in the country, in a coordinated and integrated manner. As stipulated in the National Policy of Education (1986), the AICTE was vested with statutory authority for planning, formulation and maintenance of norms and standards, quality assurance through accreditation, funding in priority areas, monitoring and evaluation, maintaining parity of certification and awards and ensuring coordinated and integrated development and management of technical education in the country.

Board of Management Studies under AICTE: The AICTE Act confers the power on the council to constitute the Board of Management Studies. It advises the Executive Committee of the Council on academic matters falling in its area including norms, standards, model curricula, model facilities and structure of courses (AICTE Act, 1987).

National Board of Accreditation (NBA): NBA was setup by the AICTE in September 1994 for the purpose of assessment of Quality and Accreditation of Technical programmes in India. The major objective of NBA is to encourage the institutions to continually strive towards the attainment of excellence. The NBA evaluation process is designed to facilitate identification of the strengths and weaknesses of the programmes under accreditation. The process is based on a set of eight broad based criteria developed through a lengthy participatory process involving more than 1000 participants concerned with Technical Education all over India. Institutions seeking accreditation of their programmes are expected to satisfy each of the criteria individually. They are expected to adhere to these criteria during the validity period of accreditation granted. They are also encouraged to periodically review the strengths and weaknesses of their programmes and strive for their continuous improvement.

University Grants Commission (UGC):The UGC was formally established only in November 1956 as a statutory body of the Government of India through an Act of Parliament for the coordination, determination and maintenance of standards of university education in India and thus, affects the management education delivered through university departments.

All India Management Association (AIMA): Founded in the year 1957, All India Management Association (AIMA) is an apex body of management with over 30,000 individual members, 3000 institutional members and 60 Local Management Associations across India and overseas created with support from the government and industry. AIMA undertakes a host of management related activities and initiatives, such as Distance Management Education, Management Development Programmes, Special Conferences, Research and Publications, Testing Services and Competitions.

Current Issues

In a research paper published in International Journal of Business and Administration Research Reviews (Jan-March 2015) current issues in Indian Management Education are identified. These are:

1 Preach-practice gap
2 Industry-institute co-operation
3 Quality of the faculty
4 Quality of faculty development programmes
5 Changing role of institutes
6 Accreditation of institutions
7 Value orientation of business management graduates
8 Admitting students without work experience
9 Issues related to placement.

Top Business Schools in India

Indian School of Business (ISB), Hyderabad: The Indian School of Business (ISB) was founded in 2001 by two senior executives from McKinsey and Company. It is a private school. Even though, it is the first business school in India to be accredited by the Association of

Advance Collegiate Schools of Business (AACSB), it is not accredited by the All India Council for Technical Education (AICTE).

Indian Institute of Management, Ahmedabad (IIM-A): Indian Institute of Management, Ahmedabad has consistently been ranked as the number one management school in the country year after year in the last several years. In its latest ranking, *The Economist* has ranked IIMA at 56 among the top 100 international B-Schools in the world that offer full-time MBA. *The Financial Times* (FT) has ranked the two-year post graduate programme in management (PGP) of IIMA in the top ten programmes in the category of Masters Programmes in Management.

Indian Institute of Management, Calcutta (IIM-C): The Indian Institute of Management, Calcutta (IIM-C) was established as the first national institute for Post-Graduate studies and Research in Management by the Government of India in November 1961, in collaboration with Alfred P. Sloan School of Management (MIT), the Government of West Bengal, The Ford Foundation and Indian industry.

Over the years, IIM-C has grown into a mature institution with global reputation, imparting high-quality management education. It has been playing a pioneering role in professionalising Indian management through its Post Graduate and Doctoral level programmes, Executive Training Programmes, Research and Consulting activities.

Indian Institute of Management, Bangalore (IIM-B): IIM-Bangalore (IIM-B) is the third IIM to be established after IIM-Ahmedabad and IIM-Calcutta. It was founded in 1973. IIM-Bangalore has the distinction of being situated in India's Silicon Valley, which is a notable advantage as compared to almost all the other IIMs. IIM-B offers Post Graduate programmes, Doctoral Programme as well an Executive Education Programme.

Xavier Labour Relations Institute of Management (XLRI), Jamshedpur: XLRI - Xavier School of Management is a leading management school based in Jamshedpur, Jharkhand, India. Established in 1949 as the Xavier Labour Relations Institute, XLRI is acknowledged as India's oldest business management school. The School's main programmes include a full-time 2-year post graduate programme in Business Management, Personnel Management and Industrial Relations (re-christened as Human Resources Management in 2011) and Global MBA, 15 months' full-time General Management programme (PGDM-GM), Doctoral Fellow Programmes and many Executive Education Programmes.

Indian Institute of Management, Lucknow (IIM-L): The Indian Institute of Management, Lucknow was the fourth one to be established by the Government of India back in 1984. It has a satellite campus in Noida for its executive programmes and is ranked among the top business schools in India. IIM-L is recognised as an "Institution of Excellence" by the Ministry of Human Resource Development, Government of India.

Faculty of Management Studies (FMS), Delhi: Faculty of Management Studies (commonly known as FMS, Delhi), established in 1954 under the aegis of the University of Delhi, offers management education to the professional managers as part-time and full-time MBA programmes.

Currently, FMS conducts the following programmes:

- MBA (Full Time)
- MBA (Executive)
- MBA (Executive) Health Care Administration
- Doctoral Programmes
- Bachelor of Management Studies.

In addition to all these programmes, FMS also regularly conducts Management Development Programmes.

Indian Institute of Management, Indore (IIM-I): The Indian Institute of Management, Indore (often abbreviated as IIM-I) is an autonomous public business school located in Indore, Madhya Pradesh. Instituted in 1996, IIM, Indore is the sixth addition to the prestigious Indian Institute of Management (IIM) family of management schools.

IIM-I offers following academic programmes:

- Integrated Programme in Management (IPM)
- Post Graduate Programme in Management (PGP)
- Executive Post-Graduate Programme in Management (EPGP)
- Post Graduate Programme in Management for Executives (PGPMX)
- Fellow Programme in Management (FPM).

Indian Institute of Management, Kozhikode (IIM-K): The Indian Institute of Management, Kozhikode is one of the 13 Indian Institutes of Management set up by the Government of India. The Institute, founded in 1996, in collaboration with the State Government of Kerala, was the 5th IIM to be established.

IIM-K offers following academic programmes:

- Post Graduate Programme in Management
- Fellow Programme in Management
- Executive Post Graduate Programme
- Social Development Initiatives
- International Exchange.

S. P. Jain Institute of Management and Research (SPJIMR), Mumbai: S.P. Jain Institute of Management and Research (SPJIMR) is a constituent of the Bharatiya Vidya Bhavan and is recognised as one of the premier business schools of India. The Institute grew rapidly in eminence from one of the three B-Schools in Mumbai in 1981 to one of the top ten B-Schools in the country by 1994-1995.

It offers following academic programmes:

- Post Graduate Diploma in Management
- Post Graduate Programme in Management
- Executive Management Programme
- Family Managed Business Programme.

Jamnalal Bajaj Institute of Management Studies (JBIMS), Mumbai: Jamnalal Bajaj Institute of Management Studies (JBIMS) was established in 1965 by University of Mumbai in collaboration with the Graduate School of Business of Stanford University. It is Mumbai University's Department of Management Studies and has been named after the noted industrialist and philanthropist, Jamnalal Bajaj.

Tata Institute of Social Sciences (TISS), Mumbai: Originally established in 1936 as the Dorabji Tata Graduate School of Social Work, TISS is regarded as India's best school of social work. The institute originally offered postgraduate diploma in Social Work. However, over the years TISS has expanded its outlook considerably to offer courses in policy planning, action strategies and human resource development. Currently, TISS has four campuses in Mumbai, Tuljapur, Hyderabad and Guwahati.

Indian Institute of Foreign Trade (IIFT), New Delhi: The Indian Institute of Foreign Trade (llFT) is an autonomous public business school established in 1963 by the Government of India to help professionalise the country's foreign trade management and increase exports.

Its flagship programme is the Master of Business Administration in International Business (MBA-IB). It is the only institute among the top-10 business schools of India that offers this programme.

Apart from the MBA-IB Course, IIFT provides various Management Development Programmes, Executive Programmes and Certificate Programmes catering to the requirements of aspiring International Business executives and mid-career professionals alike.

Management Development Institute (MDI), Gurugram: Management Development Institute (MDI) is one of the premier business schools in India. It was established in 1973 and is located in Gurugram, a commercial hub near the Indian capital of New Delhi. Its second campus has come up near Murshidabad, West Bengal.

MDI offers following academic programmes:

- Post Graduate Programme in Management (PGPM)
- PG Programme Human Resource Management (PGP-HRM)
- Post Graduate Programme in International Management (PGPIM)

- National Management Programme (NMP)
- Post Graduate Diploma in Public Policy and Management
- Fellow Programme in Management
- Executive Fellow Programme in Management
- Part Time Post Graduate Programme in Management (PT-PGPM).

National Institute of Industrial Engineering, Mumbai: National Institute of Industrial Engineering was established in 1936 as 'National Institute of Training in Industrial Engineering' by the Government of India. It is recognised as one of the 15 Centers of Excellence by the Ministry of HRD, Government of India. NITIE is renowned as the top Indian school for operations and supply chain management.

AICTE approved Management Institutes (2017-18)

1 Total institutions — 3264
2 New institutions — 48
3 Closed institutions — 23
4 Total India Enrolment — 3,94,835
5 Faculties — 55,876

Distance Teaching B-Schools

The emergence of Distance Learning Education System in our country, a few decades ago, has been a welcome development. It indeed faced its initial phase of uncertainty. Fortunately, the wheel has turned in the right direction and now this mode of education has established its credibility, competence and capability. The education system, industry and policymakers are now convinced that Distance Learning Education can play a crucial role in the emerging educational scenario in our country.

The mode of education has undergone a transformation over years. Today, it is pragmatic and dynamic. Now it is not only confined to providing course material but also offers multimedia and technology support as well as inputs to strengthen the learning process. The highly innovative, professional and technology-enabled approaches and practices have emerged in this area of education, which has completely changed the face of this mode of education.

Since Distance Teaching Education is no longer looked upon as an impediment to pursuing a course, the interest of students and several working professionals in this stream of education is growing. It has spread its roots all over the globe. It is considered to be one of the latest technologies to provide education and eligibility for employment to all, without any disparity. Keeping this importance of distance teaching mode of education in mind, we believe that it is very essential for us to highlight a few of the most reputed distance-education institutions/universities, so as to facilitate stakeholders take important career related decisions.

Here is a list of some of the well-known distance teaching B-Schools in India. The list is presented in a random order. The institutes/universities mentioned in the list have embarked upon success through their unique and innovative teaching and learning methodologies.

Some of the Well-known Distance Teaching B-Schools in India

1	Welingkar Institute of Management Development and Research, Mumbai, Maharashtra
2	IMT, Centre for Distance Learning, Ghaziabad, Uttar Pradesh
3	Directorate of Distance Education, Kurukshetra University, Kurukshetra.
4	Sikkim Manipal University, Gangtok, Sikkim
5	Lovely Professional University, Phagwara, Punjab
6	Centre for Open and Distance Learning, Tezpur University, Nappam, Assam
7	University of Petroleum and Energy Studies, Dehradun, Uttarakhand
8	ICFAI University
9	Symbiosis Centre for Distance Learning, Pune, Maharashtra
10	Amity University, Noida, Uttar Pradesh
11	NMIMS Global Access School for Continuing Education, Mumbai
12	Annamalai University, Annamalainagar, Tamil Nadu
13	Bharathiar University School of Distance Education, Coimbatore.
14	Dr B R Ambedkar Open University, Hyderabad, Telangana
15	MATS University, Raipur, Chhattisgarh
16	MIT School of Distance Education, Pune, Maharashtra
17	Indira Gandhi National Open University School of Management Studies, Maidan Garhi, New Delhi
18	Alagappa University, Karaikudi, Tamil Nadu
19	Suresh Gyan Vihar University, Jaipur
20	Bharathidasan University Centre for Distance Education, Tiruchirappalli, Tamil Nadu
21	Osmania University Prof. G Ram Reddy Centre for Distance Education, Hyderabad, Telangana
22	Bharati Vidyapeeth University (Deemed-to-be University), Pune
23	Yashwantrao C Maharashtra Open University, Nashik, Maharashtra

Choosing B-School

- Rank and accreditation among order B-Schools
- Placement record
- Level of interaction between industry and B-School

- Level of interaction between students and alumni
- Dynamic curriculum and teaching methodology
- Job-related hard (domain specific skills) and soft trainings (communication skills, problem solving skills, leadership skills)
- Faculty profile adequate and relevant work experience with respect to their domain
- Average age of board members
- Effective summer internship programmes (SIPs)
- Participation in industry conclaves and business summits
- History of B-School
- Hostel and food facilities
- Sports and cultural clubs.

Challenges of B-Schools

- Most of the syllabus in Indian B-Schools is relevant to the developed economies of the west, rather than developing economies like India.
- Though some B-Schools like IIMs, IITs are competing with the global standards and all the remaining Business Schools are not really trying to improve their course standards.
- According to a study by the Associated Chamber of Commerce and Industry of India (Assocham), 2016, about 93 per cent of India's B-School graduates are not actually employable.
- Most of the Business Schools in India are facing the problems like lack of infrastructure, poor faculty, lack of research opportunities etc.,
- The Indian Business Schools select their students largely on the basis of marks. As long as a student has got excellent marks, he/she's in. We need managers not scholars.
- Except for roughly 2-3 per cent B-Schools, it has become business with fees rising as high as 15 lakhs and the number of students in a class being more than 200 in some colleges. Only some colleges have been providing proper attention to this problem.
- Indian MBA programmes have become placement factories.
- There is a shortage of teachers at higher educational institutes. Even this is the case with the top institutes like IITs, IIMs, etc.
- A dire shortage of Ph.Ds delays in the recruitment and lack of incentives have been an important cause of the inability of the institutes to nurture the new talent.
- Problem lies not only in the higher education but from the primary education, where the low-quality education results in the weak basics of the students.

- Indian B-Schools are placement-oriented rather than education-oriented.
- Admission to B-Schools is not that hard because of the availability of management quota. This diluted value of B-Schools.
- Over-professionalisation of business is curtailing innovation.

Overcoming Challenges

How to overcome the challenges faced by B-Schools? A few suggestions are:

- Focusing on quality education, not on quantity
- Re-engineering the curriculum of Management Education
- Encourage students to take up teaching profession by providing decent salary package and ambience
- Training the present faculty members to update their skills and ability
- Students have to put through interactive, and practical sessions than mere preaching of textbook case studies
- Exposing students to industry so that they can understand the problems of the industry realm
- Provide professional training to students to focus on the current scenarios, which will groom the students take on challenges faced in the real business world
- Take action on unauthorised and illegally raised B-Schools.

Master of Business Administration (MBA)

MBA (Master of Business Administration) is a terminal and a professional degree. It is an internationally accepted masters (post-graduate level) degree with the following features:

- Imparts a strong theoretical foundation in business concepts
- Provides practical opportunities (via internships, group assignments and individual projects) to test what students learn in the class
- Builds hard skills in the area of management and leadership
- Polishes a range of soft skills like communication, motivation and negotiation
- Opens up global opportunities for career growth
- Allows MBA students to start an independent business after graduating.

Business schools in many countries offer programmes tailored to fulltime, part-time, executive course work and distance-learning students, many with specialised concentrations.

Due to the economic liberalisation in India in the year 1991, the private sector got unshackled which led to an increased demand for MBAs. Companies were willing to pay the top dollar to this new breed of executives, who were seen as wonder kids capable of putting family-held, traditional businesses on fast track. Hence, MBA became a success mantra and management became the most sought-after career for graduates. MBA symbolised status and money. Even those who managed to get into B or C grade business schools could rest assured that they had made it in life.

Different Types of MBA Courses

India has lots of institutes that offer management degrees. Few among this bunch offer quality faculty and are worthy of money paid. Given that a lot of schools offer valuable education, it is becoming increasingly difficult to make the right decision about what is a top B-School. One needs information on several parameters before one can come to a conclusion about the right MBA School.

There are lots of different types of MBA courses available in India. One can select as per their working profile and area of interest.

Masters Management

- MBA in International Business
- MBA in Operations Management
- MBA in Marketing Management
- MBA in Human Resource Management
- MBA in Hospital Management
- MBA in Telecom Management
- MBA in Hospitality Management
- MBA in Retail Management
- MBA in Entrepreneurship and Leadership
- MBA in Finance and Accounting
- MBA in Insurance Management
- MBA in Marketing and Sales
- MBA in Operations and Production Management
- MBA in Logistics and Supply Chain Management
- MBA in General Management
- MBA in E-Business Management
- MBA in Hospital Administration
- MBA in Entrepreneurship
- MBA in Banking Management
- MBA in Business Analytics and Intelligence
- MBA in Business Leadership

- MBA in E-Commerce Marketing and Management
- MBA in Financial Planning and Analysis
- MBA in Foreign Trade and Global Business Management
- MBA in International Marketing
- MBA in Investment Banking and Wealth Management
- MBA in Project Leadership and Management
- MBA in Risk Management
- MBA in Strategic Management
- Master's in Human Resources and Organisation
- Master in the Science of Public Administration
- Master's in International Business Administration
- MBA in Innovation Management
- MBA in Investment Management
- MBA in Pharma Management
- MBA in Strategic Finance
- MBA in Finance Management
- MBA in Management
- Master of Public Administration
- MBA in Business Analytics
- MBA in Rural Management
- MBA in Oil and Gas
- MBA in Power Management
- MBA in Petroleum and Natural Gas Management
- MBA in Agricultural Management.

Top 10 Qualities of a Top MBA Student

To succeed in a competitive MBA programme, an MBA candidate should have certain characteristics and here are the 10 qualities of a great MBA student:

1 *Commitment and Focus*: An MBA programme is not a cakewalk and the most successful students are the ones who are absolutely committed to the programme and to their own career goals. You should have a clear idea of why you want an MBA and what you want it do for your career. Keeping a strong focus on your goals will help you maximise your programme's offerings and give you the most bangs for your buck throughout the programme.

2 *Communication Skills*: Any effective business leader has to have great communication skills, and it certainly helps, if those communication skills are honed before starting B-School!

3 *Creativity*:Some of today's top businesses are those who think "outside the box" and develop ingenious solutions to common problems. An MBA candidate should be very creative and be

able to come up with innovative and realistic ideas for their organisation.

4 *Decision Making Skills*: A key aspect of leadership and management is being able to make effective decisions.
5 *Discipline*:A great online MBA candidate should be very self-disciplined. Not only does an MBA involve intensive coursework, but also the freedom of an online format makes it easier to become distracted worth other projects. To get a good grasp of the material and to make sure the work is being completed, you'll need to have great time management skills and be able to keep yourself in check.
6 *Entrepreneurship*: The most successful MBA students and business leaders have a strong sense of entrepreneurship. They are interested in being innovative and have a strong commitment to success. They are driven and extremely motivated.
7 *Ethics*: The most successful business leaders are those who practice with sound ethics in mind, and the ethics are key to getting through business school, as well.
8 *Leadership*: An MBA is a degree designed for those interested in leadership roles in their organisations, so the best candidates for an MBA will have strong leadership skills as well as the interest in increasing such skills.
9 *Logical Analysis*: Many MBA courses involve logical thought processes, and thus, the most successful students have a strong sense of logical analysis. They are able to think through complex situations quickly and clearly to develop smart solutions and ideas.
10 *Team Oriented*: Just as a successful business is the work of all its employees, so is the work of an MBA candidate. MBA students will often be called upon to work in teams on various projects and great students will be able to handle the group work without a problem. An online MBA student, especially, should feel comfortable working with others through email and chat programmes or even through the occasional face-to-face meeting.

MBA Entrance Tests

There are a number of National Level MBA Entrance Tests today. Various National Level MBA Entrance Tests to get into the top B-Schools in India are indicated below:

- CAT (Common Admission Test).
- MAT: The AIMA uses this Management Aptitude Test, for granting admission to its MBA and equivalent courses. MAT is a National Entrance Test.

- XAT: Xavier Aptitude Test is conducted by XLRI on behalf of the Xavier Association of Management Institutes (XAMI). XAT scores are used by XLRI, Jamshedpur and other Xavier Associate Management Institutes and over 120 B-Schools across the country for admission.
- IGNOU OPENMAT is conducted by the Indira Gandhi National Open University (IGNOU) for admission to their management programmes, ATMA.
- SNAP Symbiosis National Aptitude Test is a common written test for the admission to all the PG Institutes of Symbiosis International (Deemed) University which runs management programmes.
- IBSAT: The ICFAI Business School Aptitude Test is an online aptitude test conducted by ICFAI for admission to the MBA/ Ph.Dprogrammes of IBS, Hyderabad.
- CMAT: The Common Management Admission Test is a national level admission test for aiding institutions to select suitable students for admission in all management programmes approved by the AICTE.
- GMAT: GMAT stands for "Graduate Management Admissions Test". The GMAT is managed by the Graduate Management Admissions Council (GMAC). Admissions teams evaluating applicants to graduate programmes in management use GMAT scores as a key supplemental factor in considering an applicant's qualifications along with other factors such as undergraduate performance and work experience.
- IIFT: The Indian Institute of Foreign Trade (IIFT) invites applications for Master of Business Administration (MBA International Business) Degree Programme at New Delhi, Kolkata and Kakinada (Andhra Pradesh) Campuses.
- CUCET: It is a combined entrance test, organised for providing admission into various UG, PG and other courses offered by the central universities across the country.
- BVPB-MAT: Bharati Vidyapeeth Deemed University conducts BVP B-MAT for admission to MBA Programme.
- SAATSAAT is the Common Entrance Exam for Siksha Anusandhan University admission to UG and PG courses.
- KIITEE MBA: This is the All India Entrance Examination conducted by Kalinga Institute of Industrial Technology (KIIT University), Bhubaneswar for admission into following courses of the University.

- LPA NEST: The Lovely Professional University conducts the entrance test for various Undergraduate, Postgraduate and Degree Programmes, such as B.Tech, MBA, BHMCT etc.
- PTU MBA: Punjab Technical University PTU MBA Entrance Test MICAT.
- NIMIMS NPAT: NPAT is the official entrance test for admissions to Undergraduate Degree and Integrated Degree Programmes being offered by constituent schools of SVKM'S NarseeMonjee Institute of Management Studies at Mumbai, Shirpur, Bengaluru, Indore and Navi Mumbai Campuses.
- IMU CET: Indian Maritime University organises a Common Entrance Test.

Way Forward

Management Education is becoming increasingly important and the most sought-after post-graduate degree among graduates. Any developing country for its economic and social development requires well-qualified managers and administrators. Also, industry requires competent managers all the time, in times of secession and in times of growth. Management Education, therefore, is evergreen with job opportunities. However, to what extent our management graduates are getting the right type of Management Education. Indian Industry Survey reports that only 15 per cent of Management graduates are employable and 85 per cent unemployable. Management programmes offered by many universities and colleges suffer from serious drawbacks.

New Skills Required for Future Managers

- Information Management Skill
- Information Technology Management Skill
- Decision-making in very dynamic environment
- HRD Skill
- Innovation/Credibility
- Service Sector Management Skills
- Time Management Skills
- Stress Management Skills
- Environment Management Skills
- Entrepreneurship
- Custom Services Management Skills.

7 Hotel Management Education

Hotel Management Education is the training that is given to enrich the skills and develop the knowledge for the hospitality operations. Human Resource Management, Food and Beverage Management, Rooms Division, Sales and Marketing and Financial Management are few of the areas that are focused in the study.

One must acquire at least a Diploma in the stream to entre the career options of the field. Several programmes like Diploma, Bachelor and Master are offered in the discipline. Several courses are offered in the stream covering all the major aspects of the area. The major of them are:

- Certificate in Hospitality Management
- Diploma in Hotel Management
- Advanced Diploma in Hospitality Management
- Dual Diploma in Hospitality and Tourism Management
- Bachelor of Business Administration (BBA) in Hospitality Management
- Master of Business Administration (MBA) in Hotel Management.

Why to Choose Hotel Management as Career?

The sophistication in the modern lives made an impact over hotels of India that 20th century has seen rapid development in the increasing number as well as in the increasing facilities of the hotels. The increased number of star hotels and chain hotels is the example. These did not stick up with the major cities but also expanded to most of the major towns. Ships, airlines, resorts, clubs, guest houses, tourism companies also maintain restaurants and hotels. Thus, the requirement of the maintaining staff is also increasing day by day creating the requirement of suitable courses to supply the human resources.

There are several reasons to take up Hotel Management. Few of them are:

- Provides ample prospective opportunities
- Offers respectable as well as responsible positions
- Handsome salary
- Opportunity of self employment
- Great scope of higher positions
- Graduate of different disciplines are eligible for the course
- High chances of working abroad or on shores or other sophisticated areas.

When to Plan the Career?

The eligibility for all Bachelor courses is passing in 10+2 and for the Master's, the eligibility is bachelor's degree. Few colleges admit students considering the percentage in 10+2. But few others conduct entrance test and the admission is according to the score in the test as well as the score in 10+2.

The eligibility to the Certificate and Diploma programmes vary from college to college. Either pass in 10+2 or graduation is the academic requirements for Diploma. Few Certificate courses are offered for the Tx qualified.

What after Hotel Management?

Hotels/restaurants/resorts: Resident Managers, Front Office Managers, General Managers, Service Managers, Executive House Keepers, Food and Beverage Service Executives are few of the positions offered in hotels or restaurants or resorts.

Airlines/Ships: Apart from the regular work, one can also join in Airlines as Air Hostess or Flight Stewards. Many other positions are also offered like ground staff. The experience can also find ample opportunities in ship and work on shore.

Instructor: Many choose instructor posts in the colleges or institutes of the related, after gaining required experience and higher qualification.

Other sectors: BPOs, Hospitals, Corporate offices, Malls also offer positions to the Hotel Management students as Restaurant Manager, Public Relation Officer or Front Desk Manager.

Self employment is another best option. Restaurant, Cafe, Catering are few of the options.

Growth

The growth of tourism in India has led to the growth of hotel industry and today, the hotel industry provides a promising career to youth. Being a service industry, the motive of the hotel management lies in providing the best services to its customers. The hotel management course provides in-depth laboratory work for students to acquire the required knowledge and skill standards in the operational areas of Food Production, Food and Beverage Service, Catering, Front Office Operation and Housekeeping. Apart from these, it also imparts substantial managerial training in the areas of Sales and Marketing, Financial Management, Human Resource Management, Hotel and Catering Law, Property Management, and Entrepreneurship Development.

Eligibility

The minimum qualification for admission is the completion of 10+2. Those appearing in 10+2 final or equivalent examination can also appear in Joint Entrance Examination (JEE) for being considered on the provisional basis.

Increasing Career Options

There are innumerable openings in hotel management career. Some of the career options are found in the following areas:

- Hotel and Allied Industry
- Hospitality Executives
- Kitchen Management
- House and Institutional Catering Supervisors/Assistants
- Faculty in Hotel Management/Food Craft Institutes
- Cabin Crew in National and International Airlines
- Catering Officers in Cruise lines/Ships
- Marketing/Sales Executives in Hotel/Multinational Companies
- Customer Service Executives in Banking/Insurance and other Service Sectors
- Managers/Supervisors in Tourism Development Corporations
- Entrepreneurship opportunities.

One of the significant outcomes of globalisation is the tremendous growth in the tourism and hospitality industry. With India being one of the most popular travel destinations, the government, too is encouraging and investing in the development of these industries.

The hotel industry is a crucial part of the hospitality industry with a huge growth potential in the near future. The demand for hotel management professionals is already huge and is expected to grow more with the increasing number of hotels being set up in India and all over the world. Apart from its glamour, a career in hotel management has become lucrative and exciting, attracting more and more students to opt for it.

Hotel Management and Hospitality sector in India is consistently emerging as the best performing sectors offering several opportunities. Career360 brings an overview of the Hotel Management Courses in India after XIIth pass.

National Council for Hotel Management and Catering Technology [NCHMCT]

In order to harness the resources and also to provide a central thrust to the programme. Ministry of Tourism also established the National Council for Hotel Management and Catering Technology (NCHMCT) in the year 1982. Main objectives for setting up the Council at the apex level are:

- To advise the Government on coordinated development of hotel management and catering education.
- To collect, collate and implement international development in the area of human resource development for the hospitality sector.
- To affiliate institutes and prescribe courses of study and instructions leading to examinations conducted by it.
- To standardise courses and infrastructure requirements for institutes imparting education and training in hospitality management.
- To prescribe educational and other qualifications, experience, etc. for members of staff in the affiliated institutes and organise faculty development programmes.
- To award Certificates and Diplomas in Hospitality and Hotel Administration.

As a result of vast expansion and modernization of the country's hospitality industry, hotel management and catering education programmes gained tremendous popularity and the profits to students seeking admission to these courses. As a result, courses offered by the National Council are of international standard which have been recognised by the hospitality industry.

Hotel Management Courses

- Travel And Tourism Courses (https://www.indiacollegeshub.com/courses/travel-and-tourism-courses.aspx)
- Hospital and Health Care Management Courses (https://www.indiacollegeshub.com/courses/hospital-health-care-management-courses.aspx)
- Hospitality Management Courses (https://www.indiacollegeshub.com/courses/hospita|itymanagementcourses.aspx)
- Hotel Management Courses (https://www.indiacollegeshub.comlcourses/hotel-managementcourses.aspx)
- B.H.M.C.T Courses (https://www.indiacollegeshub.com/courses/bachelor-hotel-management-andcatering-technology-courses.aspx)
- B.H.T.M Courses (https://www.indiacollegeshub.comlcourses/bachelor-of-hospitality-and-tourism-management-courses.aspx)
- B.H.M Courses (https://www.indiacollegeshub.com/courses/bacheior-of-hoteI-management-courses.aspx).

Hotel Management Entrance Examinations

- NCHMCT JEE Entrance Exam
- IIHM eCHAT Entrance Exam
- AIUM UGAT Entrance Exam
- UPSEE BHMCT Entrance Exam
- UKSEE BHMCT Entrance Exam
- MAH HM CET Entrance Exam
- WBJEE HM Entrance Exam
- IPU CET BHMCT Entrance Exam
- PUTHAT Entrance Exam.

Top Bachelor of Hotel Management Colleges in India

1. Institute of Hotel Management, Catering and Nutrition, Delhi
2. Manipal Academy of Higher Education, Manipal
3. Institute of Hotel Management, Catering Technology and Applied Nutrition, Mumbai
4. Manav Rachna International Institute of Research and Studies, Faridabad
5. Institute of Hotel Management, Aurangabad
6. Institute of Hotel Management, Catering Technology and Applied Nutrition, Chennai
7. Institute of Hotel Management, Catering and Nutrition, Shimla

8. Indian Institute of Hotel Management and Catering, Bhubaneswar
9. Institute of Hotel Management Catering and Applied Nutrition, Meerut
10. Institute of Hotel Management, Lucknow
11. SRM University, Amaravati
12. Welcome group Graduate School of Hotel Management, Manipal
13. Christ University, Bengaluru
14. Chandigarh group of colleges, Landran
15. Maharishi Markandeshwar University, Ambala
16. Manipal University – Manipal Academy of Higher Education, Manipal
17. Institute of Hotel Management Creating Technology and Applied Nutrition, Hyderabad
18. Institute of Hotel Management, Jaipur
19. Institute of Hotel Management, Catering and Applied Nutrition, Bangalore
20. Institute of Hotel Management, Catering Technology and Applied Nutrition Gwalior
21. Birla Institute of Technology, BIT(Mesra), Ranchi
22. Manipal University, Jaipur
23. Sinhgad Institute of Hotel Management and Catering Technology, Maharashtra
24. Graphic Era University, Dehradun
25. K L University, Guntur.

Some of the Popular Colleges/Institutes Offering Hotel Management Courses are given in Annexue 1.

Annexure 1: Some Popular Colleges/Institutes Offering Hotel Management Courses

Name and Address	Course	Min. Eligibility
Blooms College of Hotel Management & Catering Technology, Om Nager, Langar House, Hyderabad 500008 Andhra Pradesh	Bachelor's Degree in Hotel Management & Catering Technology (Affiliated to Osmania University)	10+2/ Intermediate/ Graduation
Niraj College of Hotel Management & Catering Technology, 44, Uma Nagar, Kundan Bagh Area, Begumpet, Hyderabad 500016 Andhra Pradesh	Bachelor's Degree in Hotel Management & Catering Technology (Affiliated to Osmania University)	10+2 or Equivalent
Regency College of Hotel Management and Catering Technology, Regency Palace, 8-2-677, Road No. 12, Banjara Hills, Hyderabad 500034 Andhra Pradesh	Bachelor's Degree in Hotel Management & Catering Technology	10+2 or Equivalent
Shri Shakti College of Hotel Management, Venus Plaza, Adjacent to Airport, Gegumpet, Hyderabad 500016 Andhra Pradesh	Bachelor's Degree in Hotel Management & Catering Technology (Affiliated to Osamania University)	10+2 or Equivalent
Sri Padmavathi Women's Polytechnic, Tirupati Chittoor Distt. 517502 Andhra Pradesh	Bachelor's Degree in Hotel Management & Catering Technology	10+2 or Equivalent
Sri Venkateswara Institute of Hotel Management and Catering Technology, No. 11-20, Renigunta Road, Post Box, No. 54, Tirupati 517501 Andhra Pradesh	Bachelor's Degree in Hotel Management & Catering Technology	10+2 or Equivalent
Indian Institute of Business Management, Budha Marg, Patna 800001 Bihar	3-year Diploma in Hotel Management & Catering Technology	10+2/ Intermediate
Shanti Sewa Samiti's Indian Institute of Hotel Management, 11, I.A.S. Colony, Kidwaipuri, Patna 800001 Bihar	3 year Diploma in Hotel Management & Catering Technology	10+2 pass/ Appeared

Name and Address	Course	Min. Eligibility
Delhi Institute of Hotel Management & Catering Technology, Govt. of NCT, Behind Lady Shri Ram College, Lajpat Nagar-IV, New Delhi 110024	1-year trade Diploma Courses: (i) Bakery & Confectionery, (ii) Hotel Reception and Book Keeping, (iii) Restaurant and Counter Service	Xth or XIIth with Min. 50%
Guru Gobind Singh Indraprastha University, Kashmere Gate, Delhi 110006	4 years Bachelor of Hotel Management & Catering Technology	10+2 pass/ Appeared
BanarsidasChandiwala Institute of Hotel Management & Catering Technology, Chandiwala Estate, Maa Anandamayee Ashram Marg, Kalkaji, New Delhi 110019		XIIth or equivalent with a minimum of 50% aggregate
LakshyaBhartee Institute of International Hotel Management, B- 98, Pushpanjali Enclave, Outer Ring Road, Pitampura, Delhi 110034	3-year B.Sc in Hotel Management (Affiliated to EI-AHLA, USA)	XIIth Std.
LakshyaBhartee Institute of International Hotel Management, B- 98, Pushpanjali Enclave, Outer Ring Road, Pitampura, Delhi 110034	2-year P.G. Diploma in International Hotel	Graduation
New Delhi YMCA Jai Singh Road, New Delhi 110001	1-year Diploma in Hotel & Catering Management	10+2
R.M. Institute of Hotel Management N-13 Sainik Farms New Delhi	3-year Diploma in Hotel Management	10+2 with English as Compulsory subject
Rai University, No. A-41, MCIE, Mathura Road, New Delhi- 110044	Bachelor's in Hospitality & Tourism	10+2
National Council for Hotel Management and Catering Technology, Library Avenue, Pusa Complex, New Delhi – 110012	Diploma in Hotel Management catering & Nutrition/Post Graduate Diploma in Accommodation Operation and Management	10+2/ Graduate in any stream
Oberoi Centre of Learning & Development, 7, Sham Nath Marg, Delhi-110 054	3-year Diploma in Hotel Management	

Name and Address	Course	Min. Eligibility
Academy of Culinary Education, Cidade de Goa Beach Resort, Vainguinim Beach, Goa 403004	3-year degree Hotel Management	10+2 Pass
Ann Institute of Hotel Management Nova Cidade Commercial Complex, S 1 Building, 2nd Floor, Near Chodankar Hospital, PorvorimBardez, Goa	3-year degree Hotel Management and Catering	XIIth Pass
Ann Institute of Hotel Management Nova Cidade Commercial Complex, S 1 Building, 2nd Floor, Near Chodankar Hospital, PorvorimBardez, Goa	1-year Diploma in Hotel Management and Catering	SSC
Vivekanad Institute of Hotel and Tourism Management, NH-8/B, Kuvadava Road, Gujarat	Four years Degree in Hotel & Tourism Management	10+2 or equivalent with Min. 50% marks
Institute of Hotel Management, Catering and Nutrition, Department of Tourism, Panipat, Haryana	1.5 year Craftsmanship Courses: (i) Bakery & Confectionery (ii) Food & Beverage Service, (iii) Food Production	10+2 or equivalent with English as a compulsory subject
Kurukshetra University, Department of Tourism & Hotel Management, Kururkshetra 136119, Haryana	4-year Bachelor's degree in International Hospitality Business Management	10+2 or equivalent with English as a compulsory subject
North India Institute of Hotel Management, North Park Complex, Near Ghagghar Bridge, Panchkula 134109 Haryana	3-year Diploma in Hotel Management	10+2
Vatel-Oberai & Oberoi, A-23/21 DLF-1, Gurgaon 122022 Haryana	3-year Degree in Hotel Management	10+2 (CBSE, ISCE) or 1st year college or equivalent examination
Allied Institute of Hotel Management And Culinary Arts, SCO 43 Sector 11 Panchkula Haryana - 134112	P.G. Hotel Management, Degree in Hotel Mgt, Diploma Food Production/ Housekeeping/Front Office/F&B Services	

Name and Address	Course	Min. Eligibility
Institute of Hotel Management, Catering & Nutrition, Kufri, Shimla 171012 Himachal Pradesh	3-year diploma in Hotel Management (Affiliated to NCHMCT, New Delhi)	10+2
Birla Institute of Technology, Mesra, Ranchi 835215, Jharkhand	4-year Bachelor of Hotel Management & Catering Tech.	10+2 or equivalent with Physics, Chemistry and Mathematics/ Biology
Indian Institute of Science & Management, Department of Hotel Management, IISM Campus, Institutional Area, Pundag, Ranchi 834004, Jharkhand	3-year Diploma in Hotel Management & Catering Tech.	10+2 or equivalent in any discipline
AMC College, 30th Cross, 4th Block, Behind Police Station, Jayanagar, Bengaluru 560011	Bachelor degree in Hotel Management (Affiliated to Bangalore University)	10+2
Acharya Institute of Hotel Management & Catering Technology, Ist Stage, Ist Cross, Peenya Industrial Area, Bengaluru 560058 Karnataka	Bachelor degree in Hotel Management	10+2
Administrative Management College, 30th Cross, 4th Block, AMC Building, Jaya Nagar, Bengaluru 560011 Karnataka	Bachelor degree in Hotel Management (Affiliated to Bangalore University)	Passed/ appeared 10+2 with 40%
Army Institute of Hotel Management and Catering Tech., C/O ASC Centre and College, PO Agram, Bengaluru 560007	3-year Bachelor degree in Hotel Management	10+2/ equivalent examination from a recognised Board with English as compulsory subject
College of Hotel Management, A.B. Shetty Circle, Mangalore 575001	4-year Bachelor degree in Hotel & Restaurant Management	10+2
Christ College of Hotel Management, Hosur Road, Bengaluru 560029	Bachelor degree in Hotel Management	10+2
Ganga Kaveri Institute of Science and Management, # 1699, (43/1), Dr. Rajkumar Road, III Stage, Rajajinagar, Bengaluru 560010	Bachelor degree in Hospitality and Catering Science	10+2

Name and Address	Course	Min. Eligibility
Garden City College, 628/C, Ist Stage, Indira Nagar, Bengaluru 560038	Bachelor degree in Hospitality and Catering Science	10+2/ equivalent in any discipline
Hindustan Academy of Engineering & Applied Science Campus, P.B. No. 3776, Chinnappanahalli, Marathahali Post, Bengaluru 560037	3-year Bachelor degree in Hotel Management (Affiliated to Bangalore University)	10+2/ equivalent in any discipline
Indian Institute of Hotel Management & Catering Tech., ASC Centre (South) Bengaluru 560007	Bachelor degree in Hotel Management	10+2/ equivalent in any discipline
Oriental School of Hotel Management, Valley View, Lakkidi 673576, Wynad Distt. Kerala	3-year Diploma in Hotel Management & Catering Technology	10+2 pass or equivalent in any discipline
Oriental School of Hotel Management, Valley View, Lakkidi 673576, Wynad Distt. Kerala	4-year Diploma in Hotel Management (Affiliated to Calicut University)	10+2 pass or equivalent in any discipline
Oriental School of Hotel Management, Valley View, Lakkidi 673576, Wynad Distt. Kerala	B.A. in Hospitality & Tourism Management (Awarded by Queen Margaret Univ. College, Edingurh, Scotland, UK)	10+2 pass or equivalent in any discipline
Institute of Hotel Management and Catering Technology, G.V. Raja Road, Kovalam PO, Thiruvananthapuram 695527 (Kerala)	3-year Diploma in Hotel Management & Catering Technology	10+2 with a min. 50% marks in aggregate with English as a Compulsory subject
IPS Academy of Hotel Management & Catering Tech. Indore	Diploma in Hotel Management & Catering Technology	
Dr. D.Y.Patil Institute of Hotel Management & Catering Technology, Dr. D.Y. Patil Vidyanagar Sector-7, Nerul, Navi Mumbai 400706	3-year Diploma Course in Hotel Management and Catering Technology	XIIth or any other equivalent exam. With 50%
All India Shri Shivaji Memorial Society's College of HMCT, 55-56, Shivaji Nagar, Pune - 411 005	Bachelor of Hotel Management & Catering Tech.	XIIth or any other equivalent exam. with 50%

Name and Address	Course	Min. Eligibility
Mahatama Gandhi Vidyamandir's College of Hotel Management & Catering Technology, Mumbai Agra Road Panchavati, Nashik-3	Diploma in Hotel Management & Catering Tech.	
Yougantar Education Society's Shri BalasahebTirpude College of Hotel Management & Catering Technology, Shri NasikraojiTirpude Marg, Civil Lines, Sadar Nagpur 440001	4-year Bachelor's degree in Hotel Management and Catering Tech.	10+2 with min. of 50% marks
Tuli College of Hotel Management, Near Koradi Naka, Bokhara Road Nagpur 441111	Diploma in Hotel Management and Catering Technology	10+2 in any stream with min. of 50% marks
Amro Tourism Academy, " SURAJKUND" Gate No 64/3 Mumbai_Nashik Highway (NH-3) Rajurbahula, Nashik, Maharashtra 422-010 Tel: +91-253-651-1223 Fax: +91-253-237-0962 e-mail: amrocollege@hotmail.com Web: www.amroinstitutes.com Affiliations and associations: 1. Department of Technical Education, Government of Maharashtra 2. Maharashtra State Vocational Board of Educational (MSVBE), Mumbai 3. Pune University 4. Sikkim Manipal University (SMU) 5. Yashwantrao Chavhan Maharashtra Open University (YCMOU) 6. American Hotel and Lodging Association (AH&LA) of USA Name of the Group: AMRO INSTITUTES Name of the Institutes: Amro Tourism Academy Amro College of Hotel Management Amro Institute of Management	1. Three Year Bachelor of Science In Hospitality Studies (B.Sc-HS) offered by Pune University. 2. Three Year Bachelor of Science in Hospitality and Catering Management (B.Sc-HCM) offered by Sikkim Manipal University 3. One Year Post Graduate Diploma in Travel and Tourism (PGDTT) offered by Sikkim Manipal University. 4. Three Year Bachelor Degree in Hospitality and Tourism Management (BHTM) offered by YCMOU. 5. Six Month Twin Certificate Course in Bartending, Bar and Beverage Management here the student gets twin Certification: one from AH&LA of USA and the other from Amro Institutes. 6. Various Short Term Courses under auspices of MSVBE, Mumbai which are of Six months to One year Duration 7. Three/Four Year Twin Diploma in Hotel Management and Catering Technology, offered by AH&LA of USA and Amro Institutes.	Passed/Appeared in XIIth

Name and Address	Course	Min. Eligibility
Anjuman-I-Islam's Institute of Hotel Management & Catering Technology Naruddin Tyabji Marg, 92 DN Road, Mumbai 400001	Diploma in Hotel Management & Catering Tech.	Passed/Appeared in XIIth
B.V. Institute of Hotel Management & Catering Technology, Sector 8 CBD Navi Mumbai 400614	Diploma of Hotel Management & Catering Technology	
DINA Institute of Hotel Studies, No. 3, Timanna Niwas, 940/2, Model Colony, Pune 411016	2-year Diploma in Hotel Management	XIIth Std. Or equivalent
HutatmaKarveer Chhatrapati ChutheShivali Maharaj Institute of Management, Research & Rural Development, Ahmednagar	Bachelor of Hotel Management & Catering Tech.	XIIth Std. Or equivalent
Indian Institute of Hotel Management & Catering, 435, Old Station Square, Bhubaneshwar 751006	3-year Diploma in Hotel Management & Catering Tech., Affiliated to Utkal University	10+2 passed or appeared in any discipline
Institute of Hotel Catering & Studies, Jagda, P.O. Jhirpani, Rourkela, Sundargarh 769042	3-year Diploma in Hotel Management & Catering Tech., Affiliated to Utkal University	Passed 10+2/ Intermediate
National Institute of Hotel Management & Catering, 457, Bomikhal, Bhubaneswar, 751010	3-year Diploma in Hotel Management & Catering Tech. Affiliated to Utkal University	10+2/equivalent in any discipline
Women's Polytechnic, Berhampur	Diploma in Hotel Management & Catering Tech.	10+2/equivalent in any discipline
Maharishi Arvind Institute of Science and Management, Bharati Path, Ambabari Circle, Ambabari, Jaipur	3-year Diploma in Hotel Management & Catering Tech.	Senior Sec. (10+2)
Maharishi Arvind Institute of Science and Management, Bharati Path, Ambabari Circle, Ambabari, Jaipur	2-year P.G. Diploma in Hotel Management & Tourism	Graduate
Maharishi Arvind Institute of Science and Management Bharati Path, Ambabari Circle, Ambabari, Jaipur	1-year P.G. Diploma in Hotel Management & Tourism	Graduate
Institute of Hotel Management, Catering Tech. & Applied Nutrition, P.S. Road, Gangtok, Sikkim 737101	1.5 year Diploma in (i) Cookery (ii) Front Office Operation (iii) Food & Beverage Service (iv) PG Diploma in Accommodation Operation	10+2 or equivalent exam. In any stream with English as Compulsory subject

Name and Address	Course	Min. Eligibility
Asan Memorial Institute of Hotel Management & Catering Technology, Tambaram-Velachery Road, Jaladampet, Chennai 601302	3-year Diploma in Hotel Management	10+2 or equivalent
Bhaktavatsalam Memorial College for Women Korattur, Chennai 60080	B.Sc in Catering Technology & Hotel Management Affiliated to University of Madras	
Bharat College of Science and Management, Near New Bus Stand, Trichy Road, Thanjavur 613005	B.Sc in Hotel Management and Catering Tech.	10+2 or equivalent
C.M.S. Science and Commercial College, Coimbatore 641006	B.Sc in Catering Technology & Hotel Management Affiliated to Bharathiyar University	10+2 or its equivalent
Canan School of Catering & Hotel Management, 1/75 Poonamallee High Road, Nerkundram, Chennai 600107	3-year Diploma in Hotel Management	
Chennai National College of Arts & Sciences, Parthipattu, Sriperumbathur	B.Sc in Catering Technology & Hotel Management	10+2 or its equivalent
Cheran Arts & Sciences College, Thittupparaj, Kangayam - Erode 638701	B.Sc. (Catering Science & Hotel Mgt)	
Empee Institute of Hotel Management & Catering Technology, D-103 Aruna Complex, Anna Nagar East, Chennai 600102	Diploma in Hotel Management & Catering Technology	SSLC/+2 or equivalent
Food Craft Institute, Thuvakudi, Tiruchirapalli 620015	3-year Diploma in Hotel Management & Catering Technology	10+2 or equivalent
Holy Crescent School of Catering, 50, Trunk Road, Poonamalle, Chennai 600056	3-year Diploma in Hotel Management and Catering Technology	Passed/appeared in 10+2 or equivalent Exam. with 45% marks
Allahabad Agricultural Institute, Prayagraj 211007	Bachelor of Hotel & Tourism Management	
Babu Banarasidas National Institute of Technology and Management, Lucknow	Bachelor of Hotel & Tourism Management	

Name and Address	Course	Min. Eligibility
Bundelkhand University, School of Tourism & Management, Kanpur road, Jhansi 284128	4-year Bachelor of Hotel Management (BHM)	10+2 with 50% marks
Ch. Charan Singh University, Meerut	4-year Bachelor degree in Hotel Management	Passed 10+2 or equivalent examination
Graduate School of Business & Administration (GSBA), Plot No. HS-02, Block - F, Sector - Alpha 2, Greater Noida - 201306	3-year Diploma in Hotel Management	10+2 or equivalent
Institute of Hotel Management, Catering Technology and Applied Nutrition, IHM & C HOUSE, 11 R. A. Lines, Dogra Temple Road, The Mall, Meerut Cantt-250001	4-year Bachelor Degree in Hotel Management & Catering Technology (BHMCT) 3-year Diploma in Hotel Management & Catering Technology	10+2 or equivalent
Institute of Hotel & Tourism Management, C/o DevidayalAluminimum Industries (P) Ltd. 149, G.T. Road, Sahibabad, Ghaziabad 201005	3-year B.Sc in Hotel Management 1-year Advanced Diploma in Cookery & Catering 2-year M.Sc in Hotel Management	10+2 or equivalent
Institute of Hotel & Tourism Management, C/o DevidayalAluminimum Industries (P) Ltd. 149, G.T. Road, Sahibabad, Ghaziabad 201006	2-year M.Sc in Hotel Management	10+2 or equivalent
International Institute of Management & Technology, Mall Road, Meerut Cantt.	Bachelor of Hotel Management (Affiliated to V.B.S. University)	10+2 or equivalent
J.P. Institute of Hotel Management & Catering Technology, P.O Rajpura, Mawana Road, Meerut 250001	4-year Bachelor Degree in Hotel Management & Catering Technology (BHMCT); 3-year Diploma in Hotel Management & Catering Technology	10+2 or equivalent examination
Amrapali Institute of Hotel Management, Civil Lines, Nainital Road, Haldwani	4-year degree in Hotel Management & Catering Technology (Affiliated to Kumaun University, Nainital)	
Govt. Institute of Hotel Management & Catering, Dehradun	Diploma in Hotel Management & Catering Technology	10+2 with English as a compulsory subject

Name and Address	Course	Min. Eligibility
Govt. Institute of Hotel Management & Catering, Almora	3-year Diploma in Hotel Management & Catering Technology	10+2 with English as a compulsory subject
Institute of Media Management and Tech., 113/1-2, Raipur Road, Dehradun 248001	3-year B.Sc in Hotel Management & Catering (Affiliated to Bhartiya Vidya Bhawan, Mumbai)	10+2 or equivalent exam.
National Institute of Hotel Management, 29, Dilaram Bazar, Rajpur Road, Dehradun 248001	3-year Bachelor of Hotel Management	
RAM Institute of Hotel Management & Catering Tech., Niranjanpur, Saharanpur Road, Dehradun	4-year degree in Hotel Management & Catering Technology (Affiliated to Garhwal University)	Passed/appeared 10+2
Durgapur Educational Society's Institute of Hotel Management, B-312, Michael Faraday Street, City Centre, Durgapur 713216	3-year Diploma in Hotel Management, Catering & Food Science	10+2 passed /appeared
I.I.A.S., 41, Sevoke road, Near Gurudwara, Siliguri 734401	3-year Diploma in Hotel Management, Catering & Food Science	10+2
Institute of Advanced Management (IAM), AE 486, Salt Lake, Kolkata 700064	3-year Diploma in Hotel Management & Catering Technology	Passed or appeared 10+2 or equivalent examination
Institute of Advanced Management (IAM), AE 486, Salt Lake, Kolkata 700065	BA in Hotel & Hospitality Management from AIPU	Passed or appeared 10+2 or equivalent examination
International Institute of Hotel Management International, Tower X-1, 8/3, Block EP, Sector-V, Salt Lake, Kolkata	(i) 3-year Diploma in Hotel Management & Catering Technology (ii) BA Degree course in International Hospitality Mgmt.	Passed or appeared 10+2 or equivalent examination
NIPS School of Hotel Management, EC 98, Sector-I, Salt Lake, Kolkata 700064	(i) 3-year Diploma in Hotel Management & Catering Technology and Tourism (ii) Bachelor in Hotel Management	Passed or appeared 10+2 or equivalent examination

8 Legal Education

The Law Commission of India defines Legal Education as a 'science which imparts to students' knowledge of certain principles and provisions of law to enable them to entre the legal profession'. Law, legal education and development have become inter-related concepts in modern developing countries. The main function of the legal education is to produce lawyers with social vision. However, in modern times, legal education should not only produce lawyers, but it should also be regarded as a legal instrument for social design.

According to Justice Krishna Iyer, 'Profession of law is a noble calling and the members of the Legal profession occupy a very high status.' Law is the foundation of every society and it develops abiding citizens — lawyers, academicians, and aspiring judges. Legal education in India refers to education of lawyers before their entry into practice.

Aims of Legal Education

Legal education should not only produce lawyers but should be regarded as a legal instrument for social design. The main aims of legal education are as follows:

- To train students for legal profession.
- To educate the students to solve the individual client's problems as well as to solve the society's problems in which he lives.
- To provide a centre where scholars might contribute to understanding of law and participate in their growth and improvement.
- To inculcate students with operative legal rules and to provide them adequate experience to apply these rules.
- To point the right road for future development.

Thus, legal education should aim at furnishing skills and competence for creation and maintenance of a just society.

Objectives of Legal Education

The objectives of legal education may be multi-fold in a developing democratic country like India. They are:

- To develop perceptions and to understand the problems of one's society and to influence values and attitudes.
- To generate different kinds of skills and knowledge needed for tasks in society.
- To broaden opportunity and mobility in society, notably among groups who may have been deprived.
- To develop research of value to education and society with use of educational facilities.

Importance of Legal Education

Legal education is a broad concept. It includes the profession which is practised in court of law, law teaching, law research and administration in different branches where law plays a pivotal role. It injects a sense of equality before law. The standard of bar and bench is the reflection of the quality and standard of the legal education acquired at the law school. Knowledge of law increases if one understands the affairs of the state. The importance of legal education cannot be over emphasised in a democratic society. It is necessary duty of everyone to know the law. Ignorance of law cannot be excused. Thus, legal education not only produces efficient lawyers but also creates law abiding citizens with human values and rights.

Factors that influence Legal Education in India

Legal education is influenced by a multitude of factors. They are as follows:

- Governmental policy
- Bar Council of India
- University Grants Commission
- Affiliating universities
- Private governing bodies of law colleges
- National litigation policy
- Developments in legal profession
- Developments in the legal system
- The kind of students who enrol
- The caliber and commitment of the faculty
- The infrastructure available
- Technological advancements

- The developments in other fields of education
- The changes in the society.

Legal Education Institutions

Private universities have played a significant role in exploring the changes in legal education over the last decade. They engage in field of legal education and strive to improve the quality of legal education in India. On the other hand, National Law Schools lay emphasis on specialised learning. Many institutions have conferred altogether with the lecture method of teaching and have instead opted more interactive and innovative methods of learning, Law schools in India have a proliferating culture of moot courts which has made legal education far more practical and behavioural than simply learning the letter of law. The significance on co-curricular activities like seminars, workshops, etc., have now become an indivisible part of the course. Internships during the period of study are now a mandatory requirement. On campus recruitment has become a common feature of most of law schools.

Academic Degrees

In India, a student can pursue a legal course only after completing an undergraduate course in any discipline. However, following the national law school model, one can study law as an integrated course of five years after passing the senior secondary examination.

- Bachelor of Laws (LL.B). The LL.B is the most common law degree offered and conferred by Indian universities which has a duration of three years. Almost all law universities follow a standard LL.B curriculum, wherein students are exposed to the required bar subjects.
- Integrated undergraduate degrees B.A. LL.B., B.Sc. LL.B., BBA. LL.B., B.Com. LL.B. These degrees are mostly offered in the autonomous law schools having duration of five years.
- Master of Laws (LL.M). The LL.M is most common postgraduate law degree which has a duration of one/two years.
- Doctor of Philosophy (Ph.D.)
- Integrated MBL-LL.M/MBA-LL.M generally a three-years double degree integrated course with specialisation in business law.

Present Scenario of Legal Education in India

After Independence, the situation changed completely. In 1950, we adopted a democratic form of government of which rule of law became the foundational doctrine. The Law Commission of India has taken preferable steps to widen the outreach of legal education, even to the remotest corners of our nation. Law colleges are given considerable importance and the criteria are fixed for the admission procedure.

Bar Council of India developed a strategy of sponsoring a model law school with university status to act as a pacesetter for legal education reforms envisaged by its five-year integrated LL.B. curriculum. Taking note of an urgent need to bring about reforms in the university education generally, Parliament, in exercise of its legislative power under Entry 66 of List I enacted the University Grants Commission Act, 1956. The University Grants Commission Act, 1956 is an Act to make provisions for the coordination and determination of standards in universities. Section 12(d) provides that the UGC may recommend to any university necessary measures for improvement of university education and advise the university regarding the action to be taken for the purpose of implementing its recommendations. This initiative led to the birth of the first National Law School at Bangalore in 1986 which was supposed to become "The Harvard of the East" according to its sponsors. The success of the National Law School experiment was indeed a turning point in Indian legal education, particularly in respect to academic excellence, social relevance and professional competence. It soon assumed the dimensions of a movement with every state in India seeking to establish a National Law School on the Bangalore model. India has fifteen National Law Universities at present which offer quality legal education to nearly 2000 students annually.

India entering the WTO and adopting policies of economic liberalisation in the 1990s brought about legislative changes in the new millennium not only in the economy but also in the regulatory framework of human resource development. As many as six pieces of legislation are now pending in Parliament which, if adopted, are potentially capable of radically changing the higher education scenario in the country, including legal education. It is in this context that the Ministry of Law and Justice proposed what may be called the "third generation" reforms in legal education, wherein a variety of changes in the regulatory framework are contemplated along with more national law schools and additional government funding of advanced centres for research and training in law.

Factors (listed in no particular order) for the transformation of legal education in this period:

- The changing demands of the legal market at the national and global levels.
- The establishment of new regulatory regimes in emerging areas of the economy.

- The emergence of new technologies, particularly in the communication sector.
- Growth of international trade and prospects of trade in services.
- The advent of corporate culture in legal practice, particularly in intellectual property rights matters.
- The replication of the Bangalore model of National Law Schools in many more states.
- The increasing demand for legal studies from among highly talented students.
- Changes in the legal education regulatory system (Common Law Admissions Test; All India Bar Examination; the Directorate of Legal Education in BCI).
- The partnership of bar, bench and academia in the management of legal education at least in the National Law School scheme.
- Collaboration with foreign law schools and the influence of foreign-educated lawyers.
- Government willingness to finance law schools and improve faculty salaries.
- On-campus recruitment and the institution of awards for best performing teachers and law schools by law firms.
- The spread of legal publications, law reporting and legal awareness.
- The recommendations of the National Knowledge Commission (2005).
- Law school involvement in legal aid, human rights and clinical and experiential education.

Rule 8 of Chapter III of the Bar Council Rules dealing with the Legal Education Committee, enables the Committee (a) to make its recommendations to the Council for laying down the standards of legal education for the universities, (b) to visit and inspect universities and report to the Council, and (c) to recommend to the Council for recognition of any degree in law of any university under Section 24(1)(c) (iii) of the Act. The Committee is also authorised to recommend the discontinuance of any recognition already granted by the Council.

Rule 17 of the Bar Council Rules states that no college shall impart legal education unless its affiliation to any university has been approved by the Bar Council of India. Rule 18 deals with inspection by a Committee to be appointed for this purpose.

The Report of the Law Commission and concern expressed by academic lawyers and the Bar made Parliament take stock of the situation and as a result the Advocates Act, 1961 came to be enacted by Parliament by virtue of its powers under Entries 77 and 78 of List I of the Constitution of India. Under the Advocates Act, 1961, one of the functions of the Bar

Council of India is to "promote legal education and to lay down standards of such education in consultation with the universities in India imparting such education and the Bar Councils of the States". Section 49 (d) of the Act, enables Rules to be framed by the Bar Council of India in regard to the standards of legal education to be observed by the universities in India and the inspection of universities for the purpose. The Bar Council of India enacted its Rules in 1965 to deal with the standards of legal education and recognition of degrees in law for admission as advocates. Rule 21 of the Bar Council of India Rules, 1965 provides that the Bar Council of India may issue directions from time to time for maintenance of standards of legal education and the university/college is required to follow the same. Schedule I to the Rules enumerates as many as 21 directions which the Bar Council of India is authorised to give to the universities/colleges. In 1958 when the Law Commission voiced its concern there were hardly 43 institutions preparing 20,159 students for law examination. After the enactment of Advocates Act, 1961 it was noticed that there was a mushroom growth of sub-standard law schools, with hardly any regard to the quality of legal education.

Admission to these law schools was easy. Minimum marks prescribed for eligibility for admission to the law course were as low as 33% or 40% and the result was that thousands of students became eligible and all of them, including the least eligible candidate, got admission. A student who could not get admission in any other course would join law course. The quality of the teaching staff in those law schools also left much to be desired. Most of the law schools and colleges had only part-time law teachers, with an exception of a few whole-time teachers. There was, thus, hardly any commitment of the teaching staff to the cause of legal education. The sudden spurt in the number of law schools with almost free admission to law schools and the lack of infrastructural facilities and non-availability of high quality teaching staff took its toll on the quality of law graduates churned out by these law schools which in turn affected the quality of the standards of the Bar. Since many of these law schools could not house the total number of students enrolled for want of adequate classrooms and non-maintenance of teacher-student ratio, the administration of many of such law schools encouraged absenteeism. In many law schools there were more "absentees" than "present". Neither the school nor the students took law study seriously. Students could live hundreds of miles away from colleges and not only get full attendance but degrees too. Legal education as a matter of fact became only a profit-making industry. It was perhaps because of this situation that the Supreme Court in Unni Krishnan, J.P. v. State of A.P. expressed its concern and firmly laid down that "education cannot be allowed to be converted into commerce".

Now there are 101 universities in the country which are imparting legal education, out of which 91 universities are recognised and the recognition of 10 universities is under consideration. Out of these 101 universities, 24 universities have started five years' degree course in addition to the three years' degree course. There are about 500 law colleges/schools in the country. Some of these law schools are housed in small dingy buildings without any library worth the name and a teaching staff hardly qualified to teach law. To the existing number of lawyers who are about 10 lakhs, we are, it is stated adding roughly two lakhs every year. We have the second largest number of lawyers in the world next only to the USA. It is, therefore, not surprising that both Judges and responsible members in the Bar became increasingly aware of, and concerned about, the falling standards in the quality of legal education and lamented about the lack of attention being paid to this stream in professional courses. This discontent has become more articulate in recent times.

Permission to start new law colleges should not be given without proper evaluation of teaching faculty and other facilities. There should be a proper evaluation of the answer scripts in the examination. The students should be trained to draft pleadings at the college level. The standard of English should also be improved. It was also suggested that for the purpose of grant of recognition to law colleges a committee should be formed consisting of a member nominated by the Bar Council of India (and not by its Chairman only), a member to be nominated by the Chief Justice of India, who shall be a Judge of the Supreme Court or High Court and a member to be nominated by the Bar Council of India, who shall be a renowned person in the field of legal education.

The UGC also extended its full cooperation to the Committee and the Chairman of UGC in his letter addressed to the Committee on 26-9-1994, inter alia, said: "The UGC would be happy to associate with the legal education Committee of the Bar Council of India. As regards the move towards a five-year-course in law, after the +2 stage through an all-India examination, we also feel that this would be a step in the right direction in terms of improving the entry-point standards. The suggestion to grant a B.A. (Law) degree after three years to students who do not wish to practise law but may rather go in for employment is also welcome. Thereby, only those who are really keen to take up the practice in law would proceed with the last two years of education. The holding of an examination by the Bar Council of India after the five years of study with the minimum percentage of 50 to 60% being prescribed before one could obtain a license would also help improving the quality among the legal profession."

Three Decades of Reforms: Outcomes Positive and Negative

One might ask about the outcomes resulting from the influence of the above factors and the future direction of legal education in India given the level of economic development and globalisation. Never since independence has legal education received the attention it receives today from society, government and the private corporate sector. This has resulted in better infrastructure, greater private participation and increased investment, though yet inadequate for quality legal education. India today has the largest legal profession in the world (1.3 million attorneys), though not all of them are in legal practice in the conventional sense (i.e. litigation-oriented practice). If solo practice has been the dominant pattern in the past, the trend today is more towards partnerships and large firms involving multiple areas of specialisation.

Though the legal profession has been the monopoly of the male gender in the past, women are now joining legal practice in increasing numbers and are finding their places in the judiciary as well. The steady influx of people from the lower socio-economic strata to legal careers is changing the composition of the profession and strengthens democracy and rule of law in the country. Legal practitioners are finding lucrative ways to practise outside courts and litigation, compelling reforms in organisation, management and disciplinary control of the profession.

On the negative side, one must mention the paucity of competent teachers even in the best of law schools to guide the growing body of motivated students. There are vacant positions in every law school. Bright law graduates do not join post graduate studies in Indian law schools nor are they attracted to teaching and research positions in them. Many of them migrate to U.S. and U.K. law schools for LL.M. education and either do not return to India or agree to take up teaching positions in India. This situation has led policy planners to consider restructuring post graduate legal studies (the LL.M. degree is still a pre-requisite for teaching position in law schools) making it a one-year programme geared to teaching, research and specialisation (the proposal is under consideration of the University Grants Commission which regulates post-graduate programmes in law). The Bar Association of India and Society of Indian Law Firms have come forward to address the shortage of teachers, offering to send senior advocates to act as adjunct faculty in selected law schools. Some law schools have started recruiting teachers from outside India, paying them attractive service conditions distinct from the rest. Others are entering into exchange arrangements under which students and teachers are provided opportunities to learn in different environments under credit transfer arrangements. Everyone now realises that unless the faculty position is improved, the future of legal education is bleak and students with financial capacities will migrate to other jurisdictions for their education.

Measures to Improve Pedagogy and Methods of Teaching

1. *New technologies to be used in legal education*— These would include not only measures such as the use of presentations in the classroom but would also embrace web-based technologies that allow for collaboration and discussion amidst faculty and students across the country. This would also allow for the sharing of resources and enabling access to resources for students and faculty who may not otherwise be able to access them. Faculty would be required to publish the syllabus they propose to follow, along with prescribed texts and resources for students, so that there may be peer review and discussion on the same. Furthermore, the Bar Council will identify software that may be used to counter plagiarism in publications and student assignments.
2. *Measures to attract and retain better faculty*— The Bar Council recognises that the success of any reform measures, and, at a larger level, the quality of legal education in the country, is dependent upon the quality of teaching faculty at the law schools. As one step towards addressing this concern, and in accordance with the recommendation of the Supreme Court-appointed 3-Member Committee on Reform of Legal Education, the Bar Council of India has already taken measures to ensure that all law faculty are paid according to the minimum pay scales prescribed by the UGC Pay Commission.

   Further, in line with the recommendations of the National Knowledge Commission in its Report of March 2009, and the 184th Report of the Law Commission of India, the Bar Council proposes that the requirements of an LL.M degree to teach law be relaxed in the case of candidates with an LL.B degree who have an exceptional and demonstrable ability to teach.
3. *Mix of small and large class sizes for teaching*— Law Schools and faculty would be encouraged to use a mix of small and large classrooms for teaching. While large classrooms may be employed for a certain proportion of classes, it is equally imperative to encourage the use of smaller classes to ensure learning.
4. *Medium of instruction* — The medium of instruction at all law schools would be English, and this would be a mandatory and strict requirement for accreditation of the law school.
5. *Use of contemporary teaching techniques and adoption of the Outcomes Model*— The Bar Council will encourage the use of

teaching techniques employed at the best law schools across the world, such as the problem-posing method, and the adoption of the outcomes model in order to embellish language, computer, and public speaking skills, would be encouraged. Emphasis would also be laid on the outcomes model, so as to:

- Identify the desired outcomes from legal education, in terms of knowledge, skills, and professional attributes.
- Ensure curriculum design that is in line with the identified outcomes desired and enables the achievement of those outcomes.
- Ensure that students are aware of these desired outcomes, and what is expected from them in the duration of their study.
- Provide for continuous feedback to students, and guidance on how they may achieve progress in the direction of the desired outcomes; and
- Ensure that evaluation methods are accurate in measuring student proficiency in the context of the outcomes articulated.

6. *Continuous education and skill upgrades for faculty* — Institutes / initiatives for the continuous education/training of law faculty will be established to ensure that faculty are aware of, and trained in, contemporary teaching techniques.
7. *Standards for faculty evaluation*— A balance between the value accorded to research and peer-reviewed publication, and the quality of teaching in class, when evaluating faculty in law would be emphasised. The Bar Council would release guidelines for faculty evaluation, including measures such as the number of publications, as well as student feedback. Steps would also be taken to ensure effective measures are put in place against plagiarism. These parameters would be used not only to measure faculty quality and performance but would also be a part of the factors evaluated when accrediting law schools.

New Challenges to Legal Education in India

1) *Physical infrastructure and financial resources*
The law schools in India have to recognise that there is a need for creating sound physical infrastructure. There should be more funds for this and for developing research projects and other initiatives to encourage faculty members. Generally, the infrastructure of the national law schools is better than what exists in the law departments of traditional universities. Improvement in infrastructure should be across the board, including in universities which still produce most of the law graduates. University

campuses should be places that can inspire students and the faculty so that they are involved in reflecting upon the various problems that confront society. Academic freedom to think and contribute cannot be ensured if universities lack the necessary physical infrastructure and financial resources.

2) *Need for developing philanthropic initiatives*
Philanthropy in legal education is rare. It by and large remains a state-sponsored endeavour or an unimpressive commercial enterprise devoid of high academic standards. There is an urgent need for encouraging philanthropic initiatives in promoting excellence in legal education and research in the country. Recently, the National Knowledge Commission (NKC) constituted by the Union Government in 2005 submitted its first annual report. Legal education was one of the focus areas; among the different issues considered as part of the NKC's consultations with law academics and practitioners were "methods of attracting and retaining talented faculty" and "developing a serious research tradition that is globally competitive". The NKC report noted the following with regard to philanthropic contributions: "It is clear that we have not exploited this potential. In fact the proportion of such contributions in total expenditure on higher education has declined from more than 12 per cent in the 1950s to less than three per cent in [the] 1990s..." Philanthropy in legal education is essential for its growth and development. Every effort ought to be made by all stakeholders, including the law schools, the bar, the bench, the law firms and corporations for promoting philanthropic initiatives in legal education and research.

3) *Hiring good teachers and researchers*
There is a need to fundamentally re-examine the context of legal education in the country. The present system does not sufficiently recognise the key problem with regard to legal education — lack of faculty members who are good teachers as well as sound researchers. There is need to identify talent among young lawyers so that they can be encouraged to consider academia as a career option. But there could be other factors where improvements and changes are feasible: such as career development opportunities within the law schools; development of research infrastructure including the resources to organise and participate in national and international conferences and undertake serious research; a harmonious environment that fosters mutual respect; governance of the law schools in a transparent fashion.

Globalisation and the changing dimensions of the Indian economy and polity have thrown up new challenges of governance. Rule of law in all its dimensions remains the single most important challenge the country is facing. The criminal and civil justice systems are under severe stress. The role of law schools in imparting legal education and developing lawyers who are rational thinkers and social engineers is central to the future of legal education and the development of a knowledge economy in India. This can be done only if the law schools are able to attract some of the best and the brightest lawyers to make a lifelong commitment to teaching, learning, and research so that they are able to inspire generations of students to work towards establishing a rule of law society in India.

Agencies Regulating Legal Education

The Constitution of India basically laid down the duty of imparting education on the states by putting the matter pertaining to education in List II of the Seventh Schedule. But it now forms part of List III, giving concurrent legislative powers to the Union and the States. Legal profession along with the medical and other professions also falls under List III (Entry 26). However, the Union is empowered to coordinate and determine standards in institutions for higher education or research and scientific and technical institutions besides having exclusive power, inter alia, pertaining to educational institutions of national importance, professional, vocational or technical training and promotion of special studies or research.

Empowered by the Constitution to legislate in respect of legal profession, Parliament enacted the Advocates Act, 1961, which brought uniformity in the system of legal practitioners in the form of Advocates and provided for setting up of the Bar Council of India and State Bar Councils in the States. Under clause (h) of sub-sec (1) of Sec.7 of the Advocates Act, 1961 the Bar Council of India has power to fix a minimum academic standard as a pre-condition for commencement of a studies in law. Under clause (i) of sub-sec (1) of Sec. 7, the Bar Council of India is also empowered "to recognise Universities whose degree in law shall be taken as a qualification for enrolment as an advocate and for that purpose to visit and inspect Universities". The Act thus confers on the Bar Council power to prescribe standards of legal education and recognition of law degrees for enrolment of persons as Advocates. However, for promoting legal education and for laying down standards of legal education, the Universities and State Bar Councils must be effectively consulted. The University Grants Commission has in the course of time evinced interest in improving legal education and has taken various steps towards that end, through adequate funding, creating of senior posts and other means.

Commissions, Committees and Statutes

The objective of commissions, committees and reports, etc. was to give their recommendations on reforming legal education in India. The main questions before all the committees, commissions and seminars, etc. were,

- What should be the pattern of the legal education to be impacted by law colleges and law faculties of the universities to fulfill their mission?
- Should it be exclusively academic and theoretical, or should it be exclusively practical and procedural?
- Should it be meant for any research purposes of law?

First Indian University Commission, 1902
Recommendations of Chhagla Committee, 1910
Bills on Legal Education 1936-49
Bombay Legal Education Committee, 1949
All India Bar Committee, 1951-52
Rajasthan Legal Education Committee, 1955
Law Commission of India, 1958
Advocates Act, 1961
Gajendra Gadkar Committee, 1964
All India Seminars on Legal Education, 1972
Establishment of Bar Council of India Trust, 1974
Legal Education Seminar, Bombay, 1977
First National Convention on Legal Education, 1977
National Conference on Legal Education, Hyderabad, 1981
All India Law Teachers Conference, 1981
Report of Bar Council of India, 1982
All India Council for Technical Education Act, 1987
Report of the Curriculum Development Centre in Law, 1990
Bar Council of India Training Rules, 1995
Report of Professional Legal Education Reform Committee, 1996.

9 Agricultural Education

India is an agricultural country. Agriculture and its allied activities act as the main source of livelihood for more than 80% population of rural India. It provides employment to approximately 52% of labour. Its contribution to Gross Domestic Product (GDP) is between 14 to 15%. At the time of Independence, India faced food grain shortage. But India achieved spectacular growth in agriculture sector since 1966 and today India is self-sufficient in most of the foodgrains despite increase in population. The foodgrains production of India increased from 51 million tonnes in 1950 to about record 273.38 million tons in 2016-17. This growth in itself represents a remarkable achievement in the history of world agriculture. India has achieved significant growth in agriculture, milk, fish, oilseeds, fruits and vegetables owing to green, white, blue and yellow revolutions. All these revolutions have brought prosperity for the farmers. Many factors are responsible for these achievements, viz., conducive government policies, receptivity of the farmers and establishment of higher agricultural education institutions.

In order to sustain, diversify and realise the potential of agriculture sectors, itis necessary to develop skilled human resources. Agricultural human resource development is a continuous process undertaken by agricultural universities. Agriculture universities impart education in the various disciplines of agriculture: Agriculture, Agricultural Engineering, Forestry, Horticulture, Veterinary and Animal Husbandry, Dairy Science, Food Technology, Fisheries Science, Agriculture Information Technology, Agri Business Management, etc. They impart education at thelevel of diploma, degree, masters, and doctoral levels.

The history of agricultural education in India can be traced back to medieval period when study of agriculture was included in the curricula of Nalanda and Takshashila Universities as an important subject.

However, formalised courses in agricultural education began only at the beginning of 20th Century when six agricultural colleges were established at Kanpur, Lyalpur (now in Pakistan), Coimbatore and Nagpur in 1905, at Pune in 1907 and at Sabour in 1908 under the General Universities. After the Independence, the Government of India initiated an extensive planning process. To ensure orderly growth, the Indian Council of Agricultural Research (ICAR), which is the apex body for coordinating, guiding, and managing research and education in agriculture in the entire country, took the lead and drafted the first Model Act for Agricultural Universities in India in 1966 and encouraged the setting up of exclusive State Agricultural Universities for research, extension and education support. The first Agriculture University in the country was set up in 1960 at Pantnagar (now in Uttarakhand), which paved the way for establishment of agricultural universities in other states. At present, there are 73 Agricultural Universities (AUs) including five deemed-to-be universities, two Central Agricultural Universities and four Central Universities with agriculture faculty. The intake capacity of students, which was less than 5,000 in 1960, has now gone up to 40,000. With about 350 constituent colleges, these AUs enroll, on annual basis, about 25,000 students at UG level, over 15,000 at Masters' level and Ph.D. programmes. In addition to this, there are many private affiliated colleges enrolling thousands of students annually. There are about 23,000 scientists for teaching, research and extension under the present ICAR-Agricultural Universities (AUs) system. Degree courses in 11 UG disciplines and 93 disciplines at PG level are offered with an emphasis on learning through hands-on practice sessions. About 52% students admitted are from rural background and 36% are girls.

Emerging Challenges in Agriculture Sector

Presently, agriculture faces many challenges such as (i) Low productivity (averaging to 60% of world average), (ii) Decreasing profitability in farming, (iii) Rising quality competitiveness under the pressure of globalisation, (iv) Poor linkage of farms with the market, (v) Low knowledge of input for agriculture, (vi) Wide gap between lab and land experiments, (vii) Low level of mechanisation and value addition, (viii) Management of supply chain management and product lifecycle, (ix) Lack of qualified manpower to address the new and emerging challenges and deliver at grassroots level, (x) Mounting threat to sustainability arising from depleting quality of natural resources, biotic and abiotic stresses and inefficient use of agro-inputs, and (xi) Poorly coordinated natural disaster management system.

To properly address these challenges, competent human resource in sufficiently large numbers would be required in the near future. To achieve this, a renewed thrust for higher agricultural education is necessary with enhanced financial support to the ICARAU system. Estimates suggest that by the year 2020, more than 16,000 scientific manpower would be required to cater to the needs of R&D in the country. At present, there is a substantial gap of 50% or more between demand and supply of manpower in agriculture and allied sciences sector. The projections indicate that by 2020, the annual out-turn required for Undergraduate and above would be about 54,000 as against the present annual out-turn of around 40,000. This means that sincere efforts are required to attract more number of students towards Higher Agricultural Education. There is a vast scope for young graduates to undertake agriculture as their profession which is directly or indirectly contributing to the economic and social development of the country.

Recently, Indian Council of Agriculture Research (ICAR) has recognised degree of B.Sc Agri in different State Agriculture Universities of the country as a Professional Degree. Nine courses have been granted the recognition of 'Professional Degrees' namely, Agriculture, Horticulture, Agriculture Engineering, Sericulture, Forestry, Food Technology, Biotechnology, Home or Community Science, Food Nutrition, and Dietetics. With these courses now being professional, specialised requirements can be imparted as Indian agriculture is increasingly in need of micro-level attention. Fifth Deans Committee report gave terms of reference, considering contemporary challenges for employability of passing out graduates and to adopt a holistic approach for quality assurance in agricultural education. The Committee has restructured course curricula and reoriented the system to develop needed skills and entrepreneurial mindset among the graduates to take up self-employment, contribute to enhanced rural livelihood and food security, sustainability of agriculture and be propeller for agricultural transformation. The professional degree status provides a lot of benefits for students such as enhanced rate of fellowship from DBT and other such agencies. More students and their parents prefer to study in agriculture stream.

The higher educational scenario in present times is influenced by forces of globalisation, emergences of new areas of specialisation such as intellectual property rights (IPRs) and World Trade Organisation (WTO) and General Agreement on Trade in Services (GATS) related areas, cutting-edge new beneficial technologies like biotechnology, nanotechnology, etc. Agricultural graduates on completion of their studies must possess knowledge about all such new techniques. They must be able to handle the new challenges posed by globalised environment. The most important thing is that agricultural education should address the requirement of major stake holder, i.e., Indian farmer.

Career Opportunities in Agriculture Science and Technology

India is a leading global leader in agriculture and a major part of the Indian economy is driven by agriculture. Over 52% of the rural households depend on agriculture for their employment. India is one of the largest producers of vegetables, fruits and flowers in the world. Also, India is the largest producer of milk, second largest of sugar, leading producer of coconut and spices. India is one of the largest exporters of agricultural commodities such as spices, flowers, mushrooms, oilseeds, milk, rice, food grains and other vegetables. Society needs food, and hence, agriculture will always be a lucrative career option. Indian government is also backing up the agriculture sector very strongly which was clearly reflected from the budget 2016-17. In future budget is expected to pitch for more reforms in agriculture marketing and increased funds for insurance and irrigation schemes. Agriculture credit has been raised to a record ₹10 Lakh Crores. Besides Government, private bodies and foreign investors are also showing great interest in the Indian agricultural industry. As per the official reports of the Department of Industrial Policy and Promotion (DIPP), Indian agricultural sector has attracted Foreign Direct Investment (FDI) equity inflow of about USD 2.8 billion from April 2000 to March 2016. Therefore, future is definitely bright to pursue a career in Agriculture.

Agricultural science involves research and development on production, processing, productivity of crops and end-products for consumers. Major activities include improving quality and quantity of farming, improving crop yield, minimizing labour, conservation of soil and water and pest control. Agriculture sector is not only about scientific research and development. It provides roles for students with business backgrounds as well. The traditional career opportunities are there in Government departments, research and education, nationalised banks, agri-inputs industry and Government and Policy-making Agencies. The emerging sectors include agribusiness, food processing, financial sector, retailing, rural marketing, international trade, rural credit and insurance, warehousing and commodities, NGOs and KPOs. Almost half of all the professionals within the agricultural sector have got business related roles. The key areas of MBA in Agri-Business are Agricultural Marketing, Agricultural Pricing, Agricultural Law,

Agricultural Trading and Merchandising, Agricultural Economics, Agricultural Data Analysis and Farm Management. The non-scientific roles include marketing, technical sales, merchandising, economists, accountants, finance managers, commodity traders, communication and education (social services).

Many Agri-Tech Social Enterprises in India providing jobs are such as DuPont India, Rallies India Ltd., Nuziveedu Seeds Ltd., Lemken India Agro Equipment Pvt. Ltd., Advanta Ltd., Monsanto India, Poabs Organic Estates, National Agro Industry, Godrej Agrovet Ltd., Rasi Seeds. Several startups and entrepreneurs are coming up within the agricultural sector. The four Major Areas of AgriTech startup are disease and pest control, timely irrigation and soil health, aerial survey to detect anomalies, and packaging and transportation. Hence, persons from science and/or business background want to do something good for the society, and have got the entrepreneurial inclination, agricultural sector is for them.

Agricultural education in India has registered huge expansion in quantitative terms during the last two decades. At the start of this century, there were about 35 agricultural universities. That number has more than doubled to 75, of which 15 are exclusively dedicated to veterinary and animal sciences, five to horticulture and forestry, three to fisheries and one to dairy. In addition, there are some 159 private agricultural colleges affiliated to State Agricultural Universities (SAUs), besides a recently opened private agricultural university in Bengaluru as well.

Unfortunately, the above quantitative expansion has not been accompanied by any commensurate qualitative improvement. Only 58 out of the 75 universities currently have full or even limited accreditation from the Indian Council of Agricultural Research (ICAR). Only eight universities — the Indian Agricultural Research Institute, New Delhi; Tamil Nadu Agricultural University, Coimbatore; Punjab Agricultural University, Ludhiana; Tamil Nadu Veterinary and Animal Sciences University, Chennai; Anand Agricultural University, Anand; Guru Angad Dev Veterinary and Animal Sciences University, Ludhiana; Y S Parmar University of Horticulture and Forestry, Solan; and Rajasthan University of Veterinary and Animals Sciences, Bikaner —figured in the top-100 list of the Ministry of Human Resource Development's National Institutional Ranking Framework (NIRF) for 2017.

There is also evidence of declining standards of both faculty and facility in many universities and that is reflected in the quality of students coming out.

Out of the 30,000-odd graduates annually appearing for the ICAR-National Eligibility Test — a basic prerequisite for recruitment as lecturer/assistant professor in SAUs — less than a fifth manage to clear it. Feedback from stakeholders, too, reveals that our agricultural graduates, especially from the newer institutions are to be largely unemployable.

The ICAR should be made the sole apex body for regulating agricultural education in the country. As a mere registered society today, it cannot exercise powers that other regulatory bodies such as the Veterinary, Medical, Dental and Bar Councils of India are able to, by virtue of their being statutory bodies incorporated through Acts of Parliament. If the ICAR is similarly empowered, it can regulate agricultural education by mandating minimum standards for starting colleges/universities and offering courses. Not only must ICAR accreditation be made mandatory, graduation in agriculture should also be recognised as a professional degree in order to make it more attractive for youngsters.

It should be recalled when the first six SAUs were set up during the sixties, each of them was tagged to a US land-grant university: the G.B. Pant University of Agriculture and Technology to the University of Illinois, PAU with Ohio State University, Andhra Pradesh Agricultural University with Kansas State University, Orissa University of Agriculture and Technology with the University of Missouri, Mysore University of Agricultural Sciences with University of Tennessee, and Maharashtra Agricultural University with Pennsylvania State University. The mentoring role assigned to these US universities proved extremely fruitful, in terms of faculty capacity-building and preparing the high-quality human resource essential both for teaching and research.

Evolution of Agricultural Education in India

Agriculture has evolved in India over thousands of years, and early agricultural practices are well documented in *Upanishads* and *Vedas*. However, there was no formal system for agricultural education until 1877, when the first Agricultural College was established at Saidapet, which later shifted to Coimbatore. In some other parts of the country agricultural education started as a part of engineering colleges like the Bengal Engineering College (then known as Civil Engineering College), Shivpur which started agricultural education as the formal curriculum in 1898. It was only in the beginning of the 20th Century, the need for formal agricultural research and education on a larger scale was realised with the establishment of Imperial Agricultural Research Institute (IARI) at Pusa, in 1905, where the agricultural education programme of the Civil Engineering College, Shivpur, had shifted a year earlier. Pusa, situated in the heart of Indo-Gangetic plains in North

Bihar, was selected as it is one of the richest agro-ecological regions of the world. Establishment of IARI in 1905, was followed by the establishment of colleges at Kanpur, Nagpur, Lyallpur and Coimbatore in 1906, Pune in 1907 and Sabour in 1908.

Right from its inception, IARI has been developing trained manpower for the country, and training officers of the Departments of Agriculture. High demand for such trainings led to the start of formal training courses leading to two years Diploma of Associateship of IARI from 1923 to 1957. The Associateship of IARI was recognised as equivalent to the M.Sc. degree of Indian Universities by the Ministry of Education in 1949. The Associates of IARI became the backbone of the National Agricultural Research System (NARS). The Institute shifted to its present location in New Delhi in 1936, and it was renamed as Indian Agricultural Research Institute (IARI) in 1947.

Immediately, after the Independence in 1947, the Government of India formed the University Education Commission under the Chairmanship of Dr. S. Radhakrishnan, who identified agricultural education as a major issue, and recommended establishment of Rural Universities (S. Radhakrishanan, 1949). Located in rural settings, the Rural Universities were to consist of a ring of small residential undergraduate colleges with specialised main University, for post-graduate education at the Centre. The Rural Universities were proposed to be autonomous and free to develop their own programmes, syllabuses, curricula, and regulations to teach all subjects, including literature, history, philosophy, psychology, social sciences, mathematics and the natural sciences. The concept of rural University was very similar to the Land Grant Colleges. Subsequently, two joint Indo-American Teams of Agricultural Research Education (1954-55 and 1959-60) also endorsed the recommendation of the University Education Commission and suggested establishment of Agricultural Universities in various States of the Country on the pattern of the Land Grant Colleges of the USA.

In 1958, the University Grants Commission accorded the status of a Deemed-to-be University to IARI, to impart post graduate education leading to M.Sc. and Ph.D. degrees. This was the beginning of reorganisation and modernisation of higher agricultural education in the country. The newly established Post Graduate School of IARI, developed regulations with the objectives of (a) integrating teaching, research and extension, (b) promoting multi-disciplinary team work, (c) introducing flexible course credit system with continuous internal evaluation, (d) promoting organisational and operational autonomy, and (e) working towards the philosophy of service to society by solving social and economic problems, particularly of rural India.

The first State Agricultural University (SAU) was established in 1960 at Pantnagar, as UP was the only State which developed a blueprint to establish an SAU on 16000 acre Government farm (the Tarai State Farm). Government agreed to the setting up of the Agricultural University at Pantnagar only as an experimental measure. Soon, new SAUs were established at Bhubaneshwar (1962) and Ludhiana (1962), Hyderabad (1964), Jabalpur (1964), Bangalore (1965), and others. Today there are 66 universities/institutions imparting agricultural education in the country.

The salient features of the SAUs are: (a) integration of teaching, research and extension functions at all levels, (b) course-credit pattern of education with continuous internal evaluation, (c) teaching through constituent colleges with no provision for affiliated colleges, (d) organisational and operational autonomy, and other features related to overall improvement in social and economic conditions of rural areas. Later the Education Commission (1964-66) recommended establishment of at least one Agricultural University in each State. The Indian Council of Agricultural Research developed a Model in 1966 which could be adopted with such changes as were deemed necessary by the newly developed Agricultural University.

Agricultural Universities

Agricultural Universities or 'AUs' are mostly public universities in India that are engaged in teaching, research and extension in agriculture and related disciplines. In India, agricultural education has evolved into a large and distinct domain, often separately from other areas of higher education. Indian Council of Agricultural Research is the main regulatory authority of agricultural education in India, while the disciplines of veterinary medicine and forestry are regulated by the Veterinary Council of India and Indian Council of Forestry Research and Education respectively. Based on the statutes establishing these universities, agricultural universities in India can be grouped into various types:

- State Agricultural Universities
- Deemed Universities
- Central Agricultural Universities

State Agricultural Universities

State Agricultural Universities (SAUs) are the predominant class of agricultural universities in India. A SAU is usually a university established by an act of state legislature with a dedicated mandate of teaching, research and extension in agriculture and related disciplines.

History of SAUs

After Independence, one of the greatest challenges before the country was agriculture and rural development. This necessitated the availability of trained human resources in these areas. The first Education Commission of India (1949), headed by Sarvepalli Radhakrishnan, recommended setting up rural universities in India on the American land-grant model. In the 1950s, Indian Parliament was already setting up specialised engineering universities Indian Institutes of Technology as Institutes of National Importance. However, the Parliament had limited mandate in establishing such specialised institutions for agricultural education, despite the urgent need, as the Constitution of India had conferred the power to make laws in subjects of agriculture (including agricultural research and education) exclusively in the domain of the states.

The State of Uttar Pradesh (UP) took the first step for establishing an agricultural university in 1954, when it invited an Indo-American team headed by Dr. K.R. Damle, the Vice-President of Indian Council of Agricultural Research (ICAR), to consider an area around Tarai State farm in Nainital district as a possible site for a rural university. Encouraged by the favourable view of the Damle team, senior UP government officials H.S. Sandhu and A.N. Jha visited the United States to look for collaborations with US universities. In consultation with University of Illinios Dean Dr. H.W. Hannah, the State of UP presented a proposal to the central government in 1956 for establishing a land-grant style university. Thereafter, a contract was signed between the Government of India, the Technical Cooperation Mission and a few US land-grant universities, to promote agricultural education in India. The US Universities included the University of Tennessee, Ohio State University, Kansas State University, the University of Illinois, Pennsylvania State University, and the University of Missouri.

The UP Act XI-V of 1958, the founding legislative act for establishing an agricultural university was promulgated by state legislature of UP. The task of mentoring the proposed university in UP was assigned to the University of Illinois, which signed a contract in 1959. Thus, the first state agricultural university of India, G.B. Pant University of Agriculture and Technology, was established in Pantnagar (then in Uttar Pradesh, now in Uttarakhand). It was inaugurated by the first Prime Minister of India Jawaharlal Nehru on 17 November 1960. The model of establishing Pantnagar University paved the way for establishing state government supported dedicated universities for agricultural education, i.e. SAUs, in India. There are 54 SAUs in India.

Features of SAUs

SAUs are characterised by their triple mandate of teaching, research and agricultural extension. Since the initial SAUs were established with technical cooperation from United States land-grant universities, their academic programmes are strongly influenced by the American system and presented a departure from the academic system prevailing in other general universities in India. The undergraduate degree programmes of SAUs are of minimum four years' duration. Since their inception, SAUs have followed a trimester or a semester system with credit-based, continuous evaluation on a 5-point or 10-point scale. This is different from general universities, which usually follow a yearly term and percentage based end-session evaluation. As envisioned in ICAR's Model Act for Agricultural Universities, most SAUs are non-affiliating universities/However, SAUs in states like Maharashtra, Tamil Nadu, Chhattisgarh etc., have affiliated private agricultural colleges. SAUs also have territorial jurisdiction.

Deemed Universities

Deemed universities are not established by an act of independent legislation but declared to function as universities by Government of India under Section 3 of the University Grants Commission Act, 1956. As per this section, "The Central Government may, on the advice of the Commission, declare by notification in the Official Gazette, that any institution for higher education, other than a University, shall be deemed to be a University for the purposes of this Act, and on such a declaration being made, all the provisions of this Act shall apply to such institution as if it were a University within the meaning of clause (f) of section 2." Thus, the provision of deemed universities enables the central government to incorporate an agricultural university without the need of Parliamentary legislation, thus circumventing the complexities of federal division for legislative powers, which has put agriculture in the state list.

There are seven AUs under the deemed university category, and a further proposal to establish more deemed universities for agriculture was made. Most of these deemed universities are sponsored by Indian Council of Agricultural Research (ICAR) and have small academic programmes as compared to SAUs. A few of these universities, like Allahabad Agricultural Institute and Indian Agricultural Research Institute, have contributed significantly to research in agricultural science.

Agricultural Universities

Notwithstanding the limited power of the Indian Parliament for legislating on subjects of state list such as agriculture (including agricultural research and education), there are certain provisions in the Constitution of India which allows it to legislate on these matters in certain conditions, such as when the Rajya Sabha passes a resolution to this effect by two-thirds majority (Article 249) or when legislatures of two or more states pass a resolution to do so (Article 252) or to implement decisions taken in international conferences (Article 253).

Some of the older SAUs, like Pantnagar University and Punjab Agricultural University, are demanding to be converted into central universities.

Evaluation of overall teaching at the undergraduate level by a select group of students from 14 state agricultural universities.

Sometime back a survey was conducted to find out the views of the students on the teaching systems at Indian state agricultural universities. These views are listed below.

Graduate Courses

- Curriculum needs complete change
- Basic sciences such as Physics, Chemistry and Biology should be compulsory
- Introduce 'case studies'
- Introduce internship
- Teachers should have exclusive responsibility to teach, and no research
- Main courses should be taught by senior faculty
- Greater emphasis on concepts
- Must provide background reading materials
- Teachers must update their knowledge
- Periodic external assessment
- Improve teaching skills
- Inadequate use of black board
- Introduce feedback after each class, to judge the knowledge gained
- Teaching should be interactive, and allow discussion
- Elective courses should be re-introduced
- Infrastructure to be increased
- Improve library facilities.

Practical Classes

- Neglected in most of the SAUs
- Should be taken by experts
- Create interest in practical through creative exercises, like prep practical classes should be held in proper laboratories and fields
- Perform field experiments in actual farmer's fields
- In examinations students should be tested for understanding the basic concepts behind experiments
- Field visits
- Attention should be given to each student
- Need more time for lab work and field experience
- Adequate facilities to be provided
- Need for at least one molecular biology lab.

Extension

- Limited farm visits and interaction with the farmers
- Greater emphasis should be given on field demonstrations with the participation of students
- RAWE programmes should begin with the cropping season
- The time of RAWE should be at least six months
    - RAWE should not be only in the last semester as at that time students have to devote more time to course work
- Extension teachers should have contacts with a large number of farmers, so that one student is assigned interaction with one farmer
- Attach the students to a village
- Provide one acre of arable land to each student to grow crops.

Post-graduate Courses

- Faculty
    - Need to update regularly; many teachers refer to very few books
    - Should be strong in basic and practical knowledge
    - Advanced topics should not be skipped.
- **Pedagogy**
    - Provide indepth knowledge
    - Discourage power-point based teaching
    - Power-point may be used judiciously, as a support to black board teaching
    - Encourage black-board teaching
    - Teachers should desist from providing notes downloaded from the internet without any change.

- **Practicals**
  - Generally neglected
  - Teachers should be motivated to take interest in practical classes
  - Develop practical exercises directed at solving problems; tackling local problems
  - Enough time should be provided so that results of experiments are seen
  - Connect practical classes with research problems to make them more interesting.
  - Need to introduce field experience.
  - Introduce survey for learning practical problems
  - Basic and advanced techniques, through hands-on experience, and not mere demonstration
  - Organise excursions.
- **Research**
  - The guides should be able to guide
  - Course load should be reduced, to allow more time for research
  - Insufficient time for research in M.Sc, it should be integrated with Ph.Dprogramme
  - It should be on a well-directed novel problem, rather than simple routine research
  - Improve facilities
  - The problem should be field oriented
  - The labs should be adequately equipped
  - Introduce credit hours.

Reorienting Agricultural Education

The views expressed by the students are sufficient to make a change. ICAR has taken several initiatives to address concerns expressed by the students. However, India is changing and so should be the agricultural education. New India does not want to be trapped in the past. Today we need skills, not just degrees, with the ability to assimilate, adapt, apply and develop new technologies. Today we need high quality agricultural graduates equipped with problem-solving and creative skills and ability to think and improve productivity of agricultural sector. Apart from the technical and generic skills, our graduates need leadership and entrepreneurial skills to build leading teams and put innovations into practice and respond to competitive environments.

The theme of the XI Agricultural Science Congress of the National Academy of Agricultural Sciences in Bhubaneswar, 7-9 February 2013 was Transforming Agricultural Education for Reshaping India's Future.

The Congress emphasised the need for creation of a world-class agricultural system. The ICAR Vision 2030, also emphasised the need to strengthen and streamline higher agricultural education system to enhance quality of human resource in agri-supply chain to meet the future challenges through cutting edge science and technology.

There is an urgent need to provide practical field experience to our graduates. This can be best achieved by making a provision in the curriculum for internship of about one year during graduation. The internship could be in the form of attachment to private companies and/or allocating time to practise agriculture in villages. This will help the students in gaining maturity. The villages which are being adopted by the Members of Parliament across the country could provide a good opportunity for students, if a formal system of attachment is put in place, to not only apply the latest technologies in field situations but also to learn the practical difficulties for which they could find solutions.

Achieving Excellence

To achieve the goal of excellence in agricultural education, the following points need to be considered seriously at appropriate level.

1. The present structure of agricultural education needs to be practical oriented, self-employment generating, production oriented, environment friendly, innovative in approach, commercial and industry based one.
2. To achieve the above goals the agricultural education policy should be reoriented so as to impart agricultural education at pre-high school and higher secondary level.
3. Emphasis should be given to provide various job-oriented certificate/vocational courses at high or higher secondary level with the purpose of obtaining first-hand knowledge on a particular agro-business or agricultural production self-earning aspects.
4. Agricultural degree programme should be offered to the students in two modules. Module-I should offer the terminal degree in agriculture with objective of producing generalist and Module-II should offer higher education on specialised fields to serve as specialist, such as scientist, researchers or teachers on a very selective basis. For this purpose, course-curriculum should be reviewed from time to time to keep pace with the changing agricultural scenario and developing frontiers of knowledge. In doing so, the views of the stake holders should also be looked into.
5. Agricultural education should be sufficiently oriented to commercial agriculture in conformity with the globalisation

and liberalisation of economic policies in the post GATT era. Knowledge on international agriculture is also very much relevant in this regard. Our agricultural education must incorporate aspects to understand the emerging market forces, which will help effective transit in product mix and input uses. The aspects of agro-business management should be thoroughly incorporated into the agricultural education curriculum with proper emphasis on entrepreneurial development.

6. To achieve excellence in agricultural education, there is an urgent need to train the academic staff in pedagogy. Our teachers have academic distinction in the subjects but not pedagogy. Hence, this area of weakness should be very seriously addressed.
7. Agricultural education should be such that its products are hot favourite in the job market. To prepare the students to job markets — domestic, national or international — the role of students' guidance and counselling cell is vital. Hence, a training and placement cell is necessary for all educational institutions. The success of students in job markets is amply focused on the quality of education in that particular organisation.
8. For quality improvement and also to give better exposure to the teachers outside their own institute, tie-up with other national or international centres of excellence is very much beneficial for improving the quality of agricultural education.

Current Agricultural Educational policy

India's current agricultural education policy was formulated in the early 1960s with the aims of:

(a) Linking agricultural education with agricultural research and extension and in this way making it an instrument of the development and growth of agriculture. Food self-sufficiency was considered to be the major goal of agricultural growth.
(b) Generating human resources for the scientific transformation of Indian agriculture was another major element of the new policy.
(c) Strengthening the agricultural education system through the creation of State Agricultural Universities on the pattern of the Land-Grant universities in the United States of America.
(d) Creating an integrated system of agricultural education by setting up in the same campus colleges of Agriculture, Basic sciences, Veterinary Science and Home Science.

(e) Providing financial resources to the new institution through budgetary provision of the state governments and development grants of the Indian Council of Agricultural Research.
(f) Granting autonomy to the SAUs so that teaching, and research are freed from bureaucratic constraints.

Need for a New National Agricultural Education

The need for a new national agricultural education policy arises for the following reasons:

(a) The old policy has served the country well in quantitative terms. The agricultural education system provides every year on an average 1500 Ph.D., 4900 M.Sc. and 9000 B.Sc. graduates. But there is a general perception that the quality of education is not up to the international standards. In more recent years, the quality of agriculture education has deteriorated.
(b) Teaching of agricultural sciences is getting increasingly divorced from basic sciences. The emphasis is on technology and applied courses rather than on theoretical disciplines without which the progress of research comes to a halt.
(c) The country is trailing far behind in the teaching of emerging new disciplines like, Biotechnology, Information Technology, Agribusiness.

10 Teacher Education

With the advent of a broader concept of education including within its fold the total personality of the educated and aiming at his all-round development, the functions and responsibilities of the teacher have increased manifold. There has, therefore, been a shift in the character of teacher preparation from one of apprenticeship to one suited to a profession. The substitution of the word 'education' for 'training' in recent years in connection with the preparation of teachers is implicitly indicative of the shift in emphasis. The Teacher Education, therefore, is a term recent in its origin.

In the broader sense 'teacher education' refers to the total of educative experience which contributes to the preparation of a person for a teaching position in schools, but the term is more commonly employed to designate the programme of courses and other experiences offered by an educational institute for the announced purpose of preparing persons for teaching and other educational services and for contributing to their growth in competency for such service. Such teacher education programmes are offered in teachers' colleges in normal schools and in colleges and universities.

Education Commission (1964-1966) said, "A sound programme of professional education of teachers is essential for the qualitative improvement of education. Investment in teacher education can yield very rich diffidence because the financial resources required are small when measured against the resulting improvement in the education of millions."

National Education Policy 2019 has very appropriately articulated that "Teacher education is truly vital in creating the team of school teachers that will shape the next generation. Teacher preparation is an activity that requires multidisciplinary perspectives and knowledge, the formation of dispositions and values, and the development of practice under the best mentors. "Teachers must be grounded in Indian values, languages, knowledge, ethos and traditions, while also being well versed in the latest advances in education and pedagogy."

Teaching being a profession, teacher education has to be a process of professional preparation of teachers. Professional preparation is an arduous task. It involves action on multiple fronts and from a variety of perspectives. A profession is characterised by a sufficiently long period of academic training. They have to acquire an organised body of knowledge on which the foundations of the undertaking are based. According to NEP 2019, this is possible only through a long duration and rigorous professional training in tandem with practical experience in the field and a code of professional ethics that binds its members into fraternity. The new policy, therefore, stipulates that "All stand-alone TEIs will be required to convert to multidisciplinary institutions by 2025 and offer four-year integrated teacher preparation programmes." It further mentions that teacher education must give importance to developing reflective teachers with positive attitudes, values and perspective along with skills of the craft of teaching. The teacher education has to be liberal, humanistic and responsive to the demands of inclusive education.

Objectives of teacher education are as follows:

- better understanding of the students
- building confidence
- methodology of teaching
- building favourable attitude
- bringing community to school
- knowing the psychology of students
- knowing the socio-economic status of the students
- comprehensive colleges
- summer schools cum correspondence courses
- better trained professionals for all types of institutions.

R.K. Nayak and G. Devi writing on the code of the ethics in education stated a teacher's obligation to: a) students; b) parents, community, society; c) profession and colleagues.

a. Obligation towards students

   A teacher should:

   - treat all students with love and affection
   - respect the value of being just and impartial to all students irrespective of their cast, creed, religion, sex, economic status, disability, language and place of birth
   - facilitate students' physical, social intellectual, emotional and moral development
   - respect basic human dignity of the child in all aspects of school life
   - make planned and systematic efforts to facilitate the child to actualise his or her potential and talent

- transact the curriculum in conformity with the values are enshrined in the Constitution of India
- adapt his/her teaching to the individual needs of students
- maintain the confidentiality of the information concerning students and dispense such information only to those who are legitimately entitled to it
- refrain from subjecting any child to fear, trauma, anxiety, physical punishment, sexual abuse and mental and emotional harassment
- keep the dignified demeanour commensurate with the expectations from a teacher as a role model.

b. Obligation towards parents, community and society
A teacher should:
   - establish the relationship of trust with parents/guardians in the interest of all round development of students
   - desist from doing anything which is derogatory to the respect of the child or his/her parents/guardians
   - strive to develop respect for the composite culture of India among students
   - keep the country uppermost in mind, refrains from taking part in such activities as may spread feelings of hatred or enmity among different communities religious or linguistic groups.

c. Obligation towards the profession and colleagues
A teacher should:
   - strive for continuous professional development
   - create a culture that encourages purposeful collaboration and dialogue among colleagues and stakeholders
   - take pride in the teaching profession and treats other members of the profession with respect and dignity
   - refrain from engaging himself/herself in private tuition or private teaching activity
   - refrain from accepting any gift or favour that might impair or appear to influence professional decisions or actions
   - refrain from making unsubstantiated allegations against colleagues or higher authorities
   - avoid making derogatory statements about colleagues, especially in the presence of students, other teachers, officials or parents
   - respect the professional standing and opinions of his/her colleague
   - maintain confidentiality of information concerning colleagues and dispense such information only when authorised to do so.

Development

Teacher education began in India during the British rule. The introduction of English education by the British government for governance necessitated the need of teachers training to the existing and the newly recruited teachers for whom English was a new language. The initial attempt in this direction was made during the early decades of 19th Century by some private agencies in the three Presidencies under East India Company. These societies were given grants in aid to train the teachers in their schools. Training of teachers of schools gained attention as a possible mechanism for expanding school system at a low cost by using native teachers and maintaining a certain level of quality by providing training to the native teachers.

The Wood's Dispatch of 1854 opened the door for government initiative in teacher education. The Indian Education Commission of 1882 provided some definite directions for strengthening teacher education. The Commission approved teacher training programmes for elementary and secondary school teachers and also recommended separate training programmes for graduate and undergraduates. As a result, separate training colleges were established for the first time, one each at Allahabad, Jabalpur, Lahore, Kurseong, Madras and Rajahmundry.

By the end of the 19th century, the institutional structure of teacher education diversified into normal schools, secondary training schools and training colleges run by the state as well as private enterprises. Teacher education became established as a good structured setup.

Later, Sadler Commission (1917), Hartog Committee (1929) and Sargent Committee (1944) recommended several measures for strengthening teacher education. Swadeshi movement gave new dimension to teacher education aims and approaches.

By the time of Independence, good teacher education had been recognised as a necessity for all levels of school education.

Post-Independence Period

When India became free in 1947, it had many problems and challenges in all spheres of national life. It was realised by leaders and intellectuals that only education could bring desired changes in the lives of the people and make the country strong through social reconstruction.

Committees and Commissions, Policies and Government Resolutions to Enhance the Effectiveness of Teacher Education

- Wood's Despatch (1854)
- Lord Stanley's Despatch (1859)

- Government of India Resolution on Education Policy (1904)
- Government of India Resolution on Education Policy (1913)
- Hartog Committee (1929)
- Abbot Wood Report (1937)
- Sargent Report (1944)
- University Education Commission (1948-49)
- Secondary Education Commission (1952-53)
- Ford Foundation Team (1954)
- Education Commission (1964-66)
- National Policy on Education (1968)
- First Asian Conference on Teacher Education (1971)
- Bhagwan Sahay Committee (1972)
- National Commission on Teachers (1983-85)
- National Policy on Education (1986)
- Acharya Ramamurthy Committee (1990)
- Yashpal Committee (1993)
- National Curriculum Framework for School Education (2000)
- Position Paper on Focus Group on Teachers Education for Curriculum Request (2005)
- National Commission Framework for Teachers Education (2005)
- National Knowledge Commission (2007)
- National Curriculum Framework for Teachers Education (2009)
- Right of Children for Free and Compulsory Education (2009)
- J S Verma Commission (2012)
- Madan Mohan Malviya Scheme on National Mission on Teachers and Teaching (2014).

Recent Innovations in Teacher Education

There are several innovations, good practices and strategies in teacher education. Some of these are:

- ICT
- Swayam
- Swayam Prabha
- Mobile Training
- Diploma in Preschool Education
- Two year M.Ed Programme
- Three Year Integrated B.Ed and M.Ed Programme
- Swach Bharat Summer Internship
- Samagra Shiksha Abhiyan
- School Internship
- Zero Lecture Programme

- Lab Area of Diets
- Reflective Teacher
- Integrated Approach of Elementary Teacher Education
- Hoshangabad Science Teaching Programme
- Introduction to School
- Pandit Madan Malviya National Mission on Teacher and Teaching Scheme.

The above-mentioned innovations conducted in the field of teacher education brought significant changes in the area. More and more innovations in different components of teacher education like curriculum policy, planning, development and transitions are needed for its continuous growth and development.

National Council for Teacher Education

The quality of teacher education not only depends on professional, sound and relevant curriculum, but also on the way curriculum is implemented in teacher education institutions. This, in turn, depends on the expertise of the faculty, its quality, on the infrastructural and instructional facilities provided in the institutions. It is in this background, the National Council for Teacher Education (NCTE) was established in 1995 as a statutory body on the provision of the NCTE Act, 1993 within the main objective of planned and coordinated development of the teacher education system throughout the country for the regulation and proper maintenance of norms and standards in the teacher education system and for matters connected therewith. NCTE is working from its genesis till now with some achieved and some to be achieved aims. Thus, in order to make it able to achieve its vision, TE in India must undertake some reforms and modifications which are listed below:

- The NCTE needs to periodically review the existing norms and standards for the various teacher education programmes (TEPs) and create a standing committee for periodic review of curricula, as well as a norms and standards of the programmes.
- It should develop comprehensive guidelines for innovative teacher education programmes for grant of recognition.
- It should develop a new framework for undertaking inspection of the recognised institutions, with enhanced focus on process parameters, to ascertain the quality of the institutions, and take appropriate action to improve the overall quality of the teacher education system.
- Set up a Teacher Education Assessment and Accreditation Centre (TEAAC).

- The NCTE should set up an institutional platform in close coordination and collaboration with state government universities, UGC, Distance Education Council (DEC), etc., and take decisions on standards, procedures, and quality parameters concerning teacher education.
- It should notify regulations to govern inspirations of teacher education institutions. These should include eligibility conditions for empanelment as inspection team members, composition of an inspection team, time required for conducting inspection, format for obtaining the required information from the concerned institutions, and submission of the inspection report.
- In order to ensure accountability, it is essential to establish a Vigilance Cell in the NCTE on priority which would investigate into any act of misbehaviour or misconduct on part of the various functionaries associated with the NCTE.
- The tenure of the office of the Chairperson and Vice Chairperson of the NCTE should be raised from 4 years to 5 years, and upper age limit should be raised from 60 years to 65 years.
- The central government should develop guidelines regarding the manner of appointment of members of the Council. Further, the members of the regional committee should be appointed by the Council.
- The NCTE should appoint a Task Force to undertake organisational restructuring of the NCTE, and to work out its human resource requirement.

Ministry of Human Resource Development (MHRD)

MHRD (2015) made some major reforms to be followed by teacher education institutions which are listed below:

- Intensive revision and upgradation of B.Ed Courses for two years, with at least 20 weeks of classroom teaching experience.
- An integrated four year course leading to BA and B.Ed degree after XIIth class.
- Increase in intake in teacher education institutions from a unit of 35 to 50 and increase in multiples of 50 in most programmes.
- Change in M.Ed programme allowing for specialisation in elementary education/primary education.
- Change in administration of teacher education institutions to bring transparency in the application process of education courses,

Justice Verma Commission, 2012

The Verma Commission made a total of 30 recommendations for teacher education institutions and strengthening NCTE. The major recommendations are as follows:

- Government should increase its investment for establishing teacher education institutions (TEIs), and increase the institutional capacity of teacher preparation, especially in the deficit states,
- Government may explore the possibility of instituting the transparent procedure of pre-entry testing of candidates to the pre-service teacher education programmes, keeping in view the variation in local conditions.
- Teacher education should be a part of the higher education system. The duration of programmes of teacher education needs to be enhanced.
- It is desirable that new teacher education institutions are located in multi and interdisciplinary environment. This will have a significant implication for the redesigning of norms and standards of various teacher education courses specified by the NCTE.
- Current teacher education programmes (TEPs) may be redesigned keeping in view the recommendations in the National Curriculum Framework for Teacher Education (NCFTE 2009-10) and other relevant material.
- Every pre-service teacher education institution may have a dedicated school attached to it as a laboratory where student-teachers get opportunities to experiment with new ideas and hone their capacities and skills to become reflective practitioners.
- There is a need to establish a national level academic body for continual reflection and analysis of teacher education programmes, their norms and standards, development of reading material and faculty development of teacher educators.
- As a matter of policy, the first professional degree/diploma in teacher education should be offered only in face-to-face mode. Distance learning programmes and the use of blended learning material may be developed and used for continuing professional development of school teachers and teacher educators.
- The institutions capacity should be increased for preparation of teacher educators. There is a need to make a Masters in Education programme of two year duration with the provision to branch out for specialisation in curriculum and pedagogic studies, foundation studies, management, policy and finance, and other areas of emerging concerns in education.

- The idea of creating opportunities for teaching practitioners to teach in teacher education institutions, as visiting faculty, may be explored. Similarly, teacher educators could be considered as visiting faculty in schools.
- Faculty development programmes for teacher education should be institutionalised.
- There is a need for enhanced investment in promotion of research in education in general and in teacher education in particular.

Reforms in Regulatory Framework

The National Council for Teacher Education (NCTE) was constituted under the National Council for Teacher Education Act, 1993 for achieving, planning and coordinated development of teacher education in the country, for regulation and proper maintenance of norms and standards in the teacher education system. In the recent past the NCTE has undertaken various steps for systematic improvements in its functioning and in improving the teacher education system, as under:

- Based on the study of demand and supply of teachers and teacher educators of the various states, the NCTE has decided not to receive further applications for several teacher education courses in respect of 13 states. This has led to substantial rationalisation in the demand-supply situation across states.
- The regulation for grant of recognition and norms and standards for various teacher education courses were revised and notified on 31st August 2009. The applications for grant of recognition are now processed strictly in chronological order. The new regulations make the system more transparent, expedient and time bound with reduction and discretionary powers of the regional committees.
- E-Governance system has been introduced by way of providing online facility for furnishing of applications and online payment of fees. MIS has been deployed to streamline the process of recognition.
- The National Curriculum Framework for Teacher Education has been developed keeping in view NCF, 2005.
- Academic support is being provided through preparation of manual for the teacher education institutions and publication and dissemination of thematic papers on teacher education.
- Various quality control mechanisms have been developed, including the re-composition of the visiting teams, periodical monitoring of the teacher education institutions and de-recognition of institutions not conforming to the norms and standards prescribed by the NCTE.

National Institute of Teacher Education

Ministry of Human Resource Development (MHRD) of Government of India in 2018 came up with a concept paper visualising Central Institute for Teacher Education known as the National Institute for Teacher Education (NITE).

"NITE is neither expected to nor can address all the existing lacunae in the system, it however would attempt to address some of the key disconnects in the field, meet the professional requirements of teachers and teacher educators, provide policy guidelines, establish benchmarks in the field of teacher education, formulate models of curriculum transactions, develop innovative training practices and cater to the specialised areas of research and development."

Different Teacher Education Programmes Offered by NCTE

At present NCTE is offering 15 different types of teacher education programmes (NCTE 2014) and the recently released NCTE regulations, 2019 have added two more programmes. (ITEP pre-primary to primary and ITEP upper-primary to secondary) in this list (NCET 2019). This implies that presently NCTE is recognising 17 different types of teacher education programmes. A description of all the 17 teacher education programmes (detailing the duration, eligibility to get admission and mandate) is presented below:

Name of the Programme	Nature/Duration	Eligibility
Diploma in Pre-school Education (DPSE)	Pre-service/2 years	Higher Secondary with 50% marks
Diploma in Elementary Education (D. El.Ed)	Pre-service/2 years	Higher Secondary with 50% marks
Diploma in Elementary Education (D.El.Ed) through ODL	In-service	Higher Secondary with 50% marks plus two years teaching experience
Bachelor of Elementary Education (B.El.Ed)	Pre-service/4 years	Higher Secondary with 50% marks
Integrated Teacher Education Programme (ITEP) (pre-primary to primary)	Pre-service/4 years	Higher Secondary with 50% marks
B.AB.Ed/B.ScB.Ed	Pre-service/4 years	Higher Secondary with 50% marks
Integrated Teacher Education Programme (ITEP) (upper-primary to secondary)	Pre-service/4 years	Higher Secondary with 50% marks

Name of the Programme	Nature/Duration	Eligibility
Bachelor of Education (B.Ed)	Pre-service/2 years	Bachelors or Masters with 50% marks
Bachelor of Education (B.Ed) through ODL	In-service	Trained in-service teachers in elementary education who have completed a NCTE recognised teacher education programme through face to face mode
Bachelor of Education (B.Ed) (part-time)	Pre-service/3 years	Bachelors or Masters with 50% marks plus two years teaching experience
Master of Education (M.Ed)	Pre-service/2 years	B.Ed/B.A, B.Ed/B.Sc, B.ed/B.El.Ed with 50% marks or D.El.Ed with undergraduate degree with 50%
B.Ed, M.Ed (3 years integrated)	Pre-service/3 years	Post graduate degree with minimum 55% marks
Diploma in Physical Education (D.P.Ed)	Pre-service/2 years	Higher Secondary with 50% marks
Bachelor of Physical Education (B.P.Ed)	Pre-service/2 years	Bachelore degree with 50% with certificate of sports activities or Bachelor Degree in Physical Education with 45% marks
Master of Physical Education (M.P.Ed)	Pre-service/2 years	B.P.Ed or B.Sc in Physical Education and Sports Sciences with 50% marks
Diploma in Arts Education (Visual Arts)	Pre-service/2 years	
Diploma in Arts Education (Performing Arts)		Higher secondary in Music/Dance/Theatre with 50% marks.

**Source:* NCTE Regulations 2014 and 2019

11 Chartered Accountancy Education

Chartered Accountancy is the most reputed course in the commerce stream. Hence, every commerce student dreams to be a successful Chartered Accountant and wants to know how to become a CA (Chartered Accountant) in India but becoming CA is not that easy. It needs complete dedication, hard work, and passion towards this course.

Steps to Become a CA in India

The vast syllabus of Chartered Accountancy is divided into four steps:

1. CA Foundation
2. CA Intermediate
3. Articleship Training (3 year)
4. CA Final

CA Foundation

If you are planning to become a Chartered Accountant in India through CA Foundation then you are taking an assumption that you have planned to appear in CA Foundation right after XIIth.

CA Foundation is an entry-level test in order to pursue Chartered Accountancy. The course is much similar to XIth and XIIth standard (Commerce stream). CA Foundation syllabus is divided into four subjects

Paper 1: Principles and Practices of Accounting
Paper 2: Mercantile Law and General English

- Part I: Mercantile Law
- Part II: General English

Paper 3: Business Mathematics, Logical Reasoning, and Statistics
- Part I: Business Mathematics and Logical Reasoning
- Part II: Business Statistics

Paper 4: Business Economics and Business and Commercial Knowledge
- Part I: Business Economics
- Part II: Business and Commercial Knowledge

The paper pattern in CA Foundation is partially objective and partially subjective. The above first two papers are of the subjective type and next two papers are objective type.

CA Intermediate

CA Intermediate is the next level in the Chartered Accountancy journey after clearing CA Foundation. Some students who are graduates or postgraduates can also apply for the CA course through the Direct entry Scheme at the Intermediate level. The syllabus in CA Intermediate is very vast and this thing makes this level the challenging one. Generally, students are not able to clear the exam in the first attempt at this level but if they plan their studies and revision in the right manner will not only clear this level in their first attempt but also able to achieve a rank.

After the declaration of CA Foundation result, nine months will be left for CA Intermediate Exams. Clearing this level with coaching is really tough, but coaching is necessary too. Hence, one should join CA intermediate coaching somewhere.

Articleship Training

Candidates can start their Articleship Training as soon as they pass any of the groups of CA intermediate.

Candidates who have appeared in both the groups of CA intermediate together should try to complete 100 hours of IT training during this waiting period. This will save time after the declaration of the CA intermediate result. After completing IT, if possible, one should complete your OT program also.

The candidates who appeared in a single group should start preparing for the next group. If they plan articleship and next group with office, then this will really be a tough task. Hence one should complete your CA Intermediate first and then go with Articleship Training.

Some students go for dummy articleship but this is the biggest mistake. Articleship training gives a vast exposure to practical experience. Hence it is referred to as a direct ticket to the corporate world.

CA Final

This is the last step in the Chartered Accountant's Journey and the biggest challenge. After completing both the groups of CA Intermediate one can register for CA Final. Although, the candidate can appear in CA Final only when he has undergone through GMCS and Advanced ITT.

This level requires expertise in each and every subject. If you plan to complete the Company law which consists 70 marks and leave the Allied law which consists of 30 marks and clear the exam. Then drop this idea, because the Institute of Chartered Accountants of India (ICAI) wants you to have knowledge of every topic it has included in the course. The most difficult task comes before a CA Student is managing studies with the office. Hence, often students complete their classes amid the training period and go for self-study after such period and this is the reason behind low pass percentage in CA Final.

One should go for the practical subjects first where chances of the amendment are less hence start with Financial Reporting, Strategic Financial Management, and Strategic Cost Management and Performance Evaluation. This will take one year to complete these subjects. Then can choose one practical subject and one theoretical subject like DT and Advanced Auditing or IDT and Corporate and Economic Laws, and one elective paper.

One should prefer the theoretical subjects in last so that one does not forget the concepts till the exam. OT and IDT should also be completed in last as both the subjects come with plenty of amendments in every attempt.

Make sure that all coaching and first reading have completed six months before the exam. Six months should be kept aside for the revision only. During this time, one need more and more practice so that one can prepare well for the Final Exams. If possible, give the mock test also, conducted by the ICAI in every attempt which will show a true picture of preparation.

After appearing in the examinations, one should complete your MCS 2 so that time does not get wasted after the declaration of CA Final result. Beside this, one should prepare for the interview to be conducted in campus placement.

A central pillar of economic growth — money is the domain of the Chartered Accountant. One of the oldest formally recognized careers of free India, from 1949 to now, Chartered Accountancy is still going strong. A Chartered Accountant takes care of all financial accounting of a company including auditing, taxation and account verification that is required by law for each and every company, small or big.

What is a Chartered Accountancy Career?

A Chartered Accountancy career involves managing the financial accounting of a company. In addition to the annually mandatory auditing, they handle accounts, taxation and give financial advice. Only an Accountant recognised by the Institute of Chartered Accountants of India (ICAI) can carry out the auditing for a company.

Skills Required

- Analytical mind
- Strong mathematical skills
- Logical thinking
- Problem-solving abilities
- Stress-handling skills
- Patience
- Interpersonal skills
- Eye for detail
- Dedication.

Course and Eligibility

The final certification for Chartered Accountancy is given by the Institute of Chartered Accountants of India and is obtained by clearing the Integrated Professional Competence Course (IPCC) and the Final examination.

1. *Integrated Professional Competence Course (IPCC)* — The first step to receiving CA certification consists of passing a total of seven theory papers divided into two groups over a course of eight months, completing 100 hours of Information Technology Training (ITT) and a 35-hour Orientation Programme. After clearing IPCC practical training begins.
2. *CA Final Examination* —A student can give the CA final examination of eight theory papers divided into two groups during the last year of a 3-year practical training. Practical training, also known as 'articleship' under a licensed Chartered Accountant, for duration of three years is necessary to qualify for the CA final examination.

Entrance Exams

The Common Proficiency Test (CPT) is held twice a year for admission to the Institute of Chartered Accountants of India (ICAI) in the Integrated Professional Competence Course, the entry level in becoming a Chartered Accountant. Registration is available after class 10 although exams can be given only after 10+2 (in any stream although mathematics gives an advantage). CPT consists of four subjects: Fundamentals of Accounting, Mercantile Laws, General Economics and Quantitative Aptitude.

Where to Study?

The Institute of Chartered Accountants of India — The only recognised institute in India certifying Chartered Accountancy. It has five regional offices namely New Delhi, Mumbai, Kolkata, Chennai, Kanpur and 118 Branches in India.

Job Profile

The work of a Chartered Accountant focuses on the proper maintenance of all the financial transactions of a company. According to the needs of the company, their role can vary between:

1. Accountancy — Preparing and analysing financial reports
2. Auditing — Checking the accuracy of financial reports
3. Taxation — Overall taxes of the company
4. Consultancy — Financial advisory as and when required

Employment Opportunities

- Independent practice
- Chartered Accountants firm
- Consulting companies
- Government Companies
- Public Sector
- Private Sector
- Banks
- Financial Institutions.

Scope

India's rapidly developing economy provides manifold requirements for Chartered Accountants as each day more and more businesses are launched. The legal requirement for each and every company to conduct an annual audit by a recognised CA from Institute of Chartered Accountants of India (ICAI) will further boost the opportunities for CAs. Apart from auditing, CAs are in great demand as financial advisors. Having a solid financial foundation is a must for all businesses, and this is made possible by a Chartered Accountant.

Institute of Chartered Accountants of India

The Institute of Chartered Accountants of India (ICAI) is the national professional accounting body of India. It was established on 1 July 1949 as a statutory body under the Chartered Accountants Act, 1949 enacted by the Parliament (acting as the provisional Parliament of India) to regulate the profession of Chartered Accountancy in India. The ICAI is the second largest professional Accounting and Finance body in the world. The ICAI is the only licensing cum regulating body of the financial audit and accountancy profession in India. It recommends the accounting standards to be followed by companies in India to National Financial Reporting Authority and sets the accounting standards to be followed by other types of organisations. The ICAI is solely responsible for setting the Standards on Auditing (SAs) to be followed in the audit of financial statements in India. It also issues other technical standards like Standards on Internal Audit (SIA), Corporate Affairs Standards (CAS), etc. to be followed by practising Chartered Accountants. It works closely with the Government of India, Reserve Bank of India and the Securities and Exchange Board of India in formulating and enforcing such standards.

Members of the Institute are known as Chartered Accountants (either Fellow or Associate). However, the word chartered does not refer to or flow from any Royal Charter. Chartered Accountants are subject to a published Code of Ethics and professional standards, violation of which is subject to disciplinary action. Only a member of ICAI can be appointed as statutory auditor of a company under the Companies Act, 2013. The management of the Institute is vested with its Council with the president acting as its Chief Executive Authority. A person can become a member of the ICAI by taking prescribed examinations and undergoing three years of practical training. The membership course is well known for its rigorous standards. The ICAI has entered into mutual recognition agreements with other professional accounting bodies worldwide for reciprocal membership recognition. The ICAI is one of the founder members of the International Federation of Accountants (IFAC), South Asian Federation of Accountants (SAFA), and Confederation of Asian and Pacific Accountants (CAPA). The ICAI was formerly the provisional jurisdiction for XBRL International in India. In 2010, it promoted Xtensible Business Reporting Language (XBRL) India as a section 25 company (now section 8 of Companies Act, 2013) to take over this responsibility from it. Now, Xtensible Business Reporting Language (XBRL) India is an established jurisdiction of XBRL International Inc.

Members

Members of the Institute are known as Chartered Accountants. Becoming a member requires passing the prescribed examinations, three years of practical training (known as articleship) and meeting other requirements under the Act and Regulations. A member of the ICAI can use the title CA before his/her name. A member of the ICAI may either be an Associate Chartered Accountant (A.C.A.) or a Fellow Chartered Accountant (F.C.A.) based on his experience. Further based on holding Certificate of Practice, they may also be classified as practising and non-practising Chartered Accountants. As of December 2017, the Institute has 2,80,221 members out of which 1,89,707 are Associates and 90,514 are Fellows. The B.N. Chaturvedi Family is credited to be the only family in India to be Chartered Accountants in five Generations.

Associates and Fellows

Any person who is granted membership of the Institute becomes an Associate Chartered Accountant and is entitled to use the letters A.C.A. after his name. Generally, associates are members of the Institute with less than five years of membership after which they become entitled to apply for being a fellow member. Some associate members, particularly those not in practice, often voluntarily chose not to apply to be a fellow due to a variety of reasons.

An associate member who has been in continuous practice in India or has worked for a commercial or government organisation for at least five years and meets other conditions as prescribed can apply to the Institute to get designated as a "Fellow". A fellow Chartered Accountant is entitled to use the letters FCA after his name. Responsibilities and voting rights of both types of members remain the same but only fellows can be elected to the Council and Regional Councils of the ICAI. Fellows are perceived as enjoying a higher status due to their long professional experience.

Practising Chartered Accountants

Any member wanting to engage in public practice has to first apply for and obtain a Certificate of Practice from the Council of the ICAI. Only members holding a Certificate of Practice may act as auditors or certify documents required by various tax and financial regulatory authorities in India. Once a member obtains a Certificate of Practice, his responsibility to the society increases manifold. The ethical principles applicable to a practicing CA provided in the first and second schedule of the Chartered Accountants Act, 1949 are more rigorous than the ones applicable to non-practising CAs or both.

In India, an individual Chartered Accountant, a firm or a Limited Liability Partnership of Chartered Accountants can practise the profession of Chartered Accountancy.

Role of Chartered Accountants

Chartered Accountants enjoy a statutory monopoly in audit of financial statements under the Companies Act, 2013, Income Tax Act, 1961 and various other statutes in India. Financial statements audited by a chartered accountant are presumed to have been prepared according to GAAP in India.

Council of the Institute

The management of the affairs of the Institute is undertaken by a council constituted under the Chartered Accountants Act, 1949. The council consists of 32 elected fellow members and up to eight members nominated by the Government of India. The elected members of the council are elected under the single transferable vote system by the members of the Institute. The council is re-elected every three years. The council elects two of its members to be president and vice-president who hold office for one year. The president is the chief executive authority of the council.

Courses for Members

The ICAI provides various professional certifications for its members. Some of them are as follows:

- Certificate Course on GST
- Certificate Course on Arbitration, Mediation & Conciliation
- Certificate Course on Anti Money laundering Laws (Anti- Money Laundering Specialist)
- Certificate Course on Cooperatives
- Certificate Course on Not-for-Profit Organisations (NPOs)
- Certificate Course on Wealth Management and Financial Planning
- Certificate Course on Enterprise Risk Management
- Certificate Course on Concurrent Audit of Banks
- Certificate Course on Internal Audit
- Certificate Course on Master in Business Finance
- Certificate Course on International Taxation

- Certificate Course on Forensic Accounting and Fraud Detection
- Certificate Course on Indian Accounting Standards (Ind AS)
- Certificate Course on Forex and Treasury Management
- Certificate Course on Derivatives
- Certificate Course on Valuation.

Post-qualification courses

- Information Systems Audit (ISA)
- Post Qualification Diploma in International Taxation
- Diploma in Insurance and Risk Management (DIRM)
- Management Accountancy Course (MAC)/Corporate Management Course (CMC)/Tax Management Course (TMC)
- International Trade Laws and World Trade Organisation (ITL & WTO).

Technical Standards

The ICAI formulates and issues technical standards to be followed by Chartered Accountants and others. Non-compliance of these standards by the members will lead to disciplinary action against them. The technical standards issued by the ICAI include Accounting Standards, Engagement, and Quality Control Standards, Standards on Internal Audit, Corporate Affairs Standard, Accounting Standards for Local Bodies, etc.

12 Journalism Education

Journalism education in India is framed in the higher education system, comprising of programmes in the universities, both government-supported and media-backed private institutions, as well as in-service and short-term courses offered by press associations and other organisations. They are offered at different levels from certificate to diploma to both undergraduates and postgraduates. Due to requirements of the media industry, there is a constant friction about the need to balance the academic and professional aspects in the curriculum. This has led to scepticism in the past about the relevance of formal journalism education. However, with globalisation and growth of the media sector, there is an enhanced need for professionals.

The information and communication revolution in India has been identified as the new pathway to national development. A phenomenal expansion of information and communication infrastructure with citizens' desire to access information, from every possible source, for furthering their socio-economic, political and development-oriented initiatives, have paved the way for growth and development of journalism and mass communication as a subject of profession. As India developed economically and gained importance its place among the emerging nations, the need of journalism education began to be realised by media in particular, and academic world in general. Journalism in India has undergone radical changes since economic restructuring initiated in 1991. Keeping pace with the profession, the educational standard of journalism and mass communication has also grown extensively.

In India, the birth of journalism education dates back to 1941 in Lahore's Punjab University (now in Pakistan) by late Prof. P.P. Singh, as an evening part-time one-year diploma in journalism course, functioned there in a somewhat uncertain permanent state. While India's partition was a setback to its progress, the department of journalism in

Lahore moved after seven years to New Delhi in 1948. Since then, this profession has seen steady progress. In January 1948, the University of Calcutta introduced journalism a subject in its academic curriculum. Immediately after, journalism courses started in Osmania University (Andhra Pradesh) and Nagpur University (Maharastra). In earlier days of journalism education, several Indian students who had gone to foreign countries for higher studies in journalism, on their return to India suggested curriculum revisions. The subject has travelled long journey facing innumerable trials and tribulations. During 1960s and 1970s several Indian universities started courses in journalism and the recognition of the course at the university level underwent drastically. Some American Universities also offered collaboration for advancement of journalism programmes to their Indian counterparts. Osmania University and Nagpur University were the examples.

The establishment of Indian Institute of Mass Communication (IIMC) at New Delhi with the support of UNESCO in 1965 landmarked media and communication education in the country. Now, the education has completed 70 years of its birth. During this period, the number of educational institutions providing journalism education has grown manifold in terms of quantity, quality and students' enrolment. A gradual change from professional to academic-oriented and western pattern to Indianised system in the education curriculum are some of the glorious symbols of achievements of the Indian journalism and mass communication education.

Presently, about 300 journalism and mass communication departments in various Indian universities (including some private and deemed universities) are engaged in providing post-graduate diploma, degree, M.Phil., doctoral, and post-doctoral programmes. Besides, over half-a-thousand institutions are offering diploma and certificate programmes in various branches of journalism and mass communication. Another development in the past one decade has been the growth of the colleges offering undergraduate courses at various private and public academic institutions. They are offered as self-financed vocational courses. All these have changed the entire orientation of the courses towards making journalism more skill course rather than one with a theoretical base. At present, more than 20,000 students pass out from these universities and institutions with diverse specialisation in print, electronic, public relations, advertising, film, media management, media law and ethics, etc.

The rapid development scenario in the field of journalism emphasises the importance of journalism and mass communication education and appropriate training of journalists (including broadcasters and social communicators), duly integrated with national development objectives incorporating social orientation. This education has been marked by a growing sense of professionalism, mainly due to four major factors. These are:

- an increasing organisation of working journalists.
- specialised education in journalism.
- a growing body of literature dealing with history, problems and techniques of mass communication; and
- an increasing sense of social responsibility on the part of journalists. Idealistic motives have also contributed a lot to the development of modern Indian journalism.

Boom in Indian Media Market

The beginning of Indian economic liberalisation in 1991 and opening up the gateway for foreign investment, particularly in information technology (IT) and communication sectors have resulted manifold growth in both the areas and revolutionised the information transmission, distribution and information consumption behaviour of the people. The introduction of foreign media channels and setting up of private media channels has widened the scope and opportunity for journalism and communication professionals. Similarly, each year at least half a dozen thousand students enter the profession and get absorbed in newspaper industry, news agencies, radio and television organisations, and other government and private organisations in the information and public relations jobs. Furthermore, the revolution in electronic media and IT and spurt in both regional and national streams of the print media have also contributed to better training of communication professionals, turning them into excellent social communicators and responsible journalists.

The growing literacy and the improvement in the lifestyle of the people of India are partially considered as the media's contribution in disguise. Since Independence, the media, particularly the press, has been growing constantly. There were 3,330 newspapers and periodicals published at the time of Independence; this number rose to 82,237 in 2010-11, i.e., above twenty-five times in 62 years. Today, India ranks among the top five newspaper production countries in the world. In 2010-11, the total circulation of Indian press (a combined total of all 96 languages) stood at 32,92,04,841 copies (Registrar of Newspapers for India (RNI), 2011). The availability of a large number of dailies/weeklies provides the reader a variety of options and choices. Scope and opportunity for press practitioners in urban sector is quite encouraging than the rural sector because maximum press establishments are located in large cities and towns and a low-rate readership in rural areas.

With the dawn on the 21st century, setting aside all debates on the issue, in the mid-phase of 2002, the Indian press has entered the liberalisation phase with government's decision to open up for the print media to foreign direct investment (FDI). This landmark decision, pertaining to the Indian press, is a measure of India's growing confidence. Initially, foreign direct investment up to 26 per cent was allowed in news and current affairs publications including business publications while up to 74 per cent in technical, medical and other specialised journals. Later, the government has decided to raise the limit of FDI from 26 per cent to 49 per cent in news and current affairs publications.

In recent years, the information and broadcasting sector has been also undertaking major changes mainly due to technological developments. Use of IT and computers has revolutionised profoundly the collection and dissemination of news and information and broadcasting of entertainment programmes. Presently, about 99.1 per cent of the country's population and 91.2 per cent of the country's geographical area is within the reach of radio broadcasting. The number of radio broadcasting stations has risen from just six at the time of Independence to 231 at present and by the completion of this current Plan period some more stations will become operational. In rural sector the radio still has good audience, whereas in urban sector, the audience is gradually declining, with the exception of FM listeners in cities and metros. The gradual decline of this, once all important media, has evoked strong response from the concerned agencies. The government has now installed more than one FM channel in several metro cities and is planning to install at least one in some other areas. Recently, the government has approved increasing the FDI limit in FM sector from 20 to 26 per cent. As on March 2011, there were 245 private radio stations and 108 community radio stations operational.

Utilisation of technological developments for citizens' benefit and to gain more popularity of radio broadcasting in non-urban sectors, the government has initiated several steps among one such is community radio and expansion of Phase-III of FM broadcasting. Likewise, the medium wave programmes are also being made more popular than before. India has crossed the 100 million mark for pay-TV subscribers, representing more than 70 per cent of TV households. According to India Digital TV Forecast report, there is still plenty of growth to come with 139 million pay-TV subscribers forecast for 2016. The number of TV homes in India grew from 120 million in 2007 to 148 million in 2011. Cable reaches 94 million homes with 88 million analog connections and six million digital ones, while DTH has commanded 41 million subscribers. As per a recent report from Paris-based international research and analysis firm Euroconsult, the satellite pay-TV industry India and some other emerging markets will help the satellite pay-TV industry attain annual global revenue of USD 150 billion by 2021, from close to USD 90 billion in 2011. The report further noted that 'Asia has become the leading region in terms of subscriptions thanks to the booming Indian market'. Euroconsult said an expected 77 per cent of worldwide pay TV subscribers could be located in emerging regions (including India, Brazil and Russia) by 2021, as against 60 per cent in 2011. The Indian television (Doordarshan) through its network of 1,415 terrestrial transmitters reaches over 92 per cent of the country's population and the entire country is also covered by Doordarshan DTH service. A wide network of private and government television companies in India have established enormous opportunities for journalistic and artistic professionals to explore their capabilities.

The cable television was introduced in Indian subcontinent two decades ago. Its rapid spread in both urban and rural areas has widened the audience, who now has more options and choices to view different channels and programmes. In our country, more than 1,00,000 cable operators are doing good business in information and entertainment, which has emerged as a major industry and also as a major cultural force. India is looked upon as an alluring market for broadcasters. Some 550 or more private and foreign satellite channels, ranging from small Tamil language channels in southern India to international channels like CNN, CNBC, National Geographic, Discovery, Times, BBC, IBN broadcasting, etc. are now vying to reach Indian viewers. According to Pioneer Invest Corp, the Indian cable industry is worth 270 billion rupees and is the third largest in the world after television in People's Republic of China and television in the United States.

Today, among the major Asian industrialised countries, India has abundant technically skilled manpower and is significantly contributing this skilled manpower towards global IT development. The computer, communication and control, commonly called 3Cs, are going to drive the country's economy and overall development in rapid manner achieving the desired growth in only a decade compared to the growth achieved by it during the past five decades or more. IT is the fastest growing industrial segment in India and has had an impact on almost every field of activity in recent years. During the last decade, the IT sector in our country registered an unprecedented growth. The hyperbole of internet and World Wide Web (WWW) is gradually changing

Indians' living, talking and interacting behaviour and is expected to change some of the fundamental features of the way we operate. The major areas of this revolution, such as broadcasting, telecommunication, media, military, computers and contents, etc., have shown high growth of penetration in the country only during the last decade. India is one of the fastest growing PC market and internet usages in the Asia-Pacific region. Personal computer (PC) in India is estimated to have crossed 52 million units as of the end of 2010. The current installed base of personal computer translates into one computer for every 25 Indians, doubling the per capita PC availability in just four years. It may be recalled that at the end of 2006 there was approximately one computer for every 50 Indians.

The growth of PC market combined with infrastructural developments in telecommunication sector has accelerated the internet penetration faster in India. According to a study by the Internet and Mobile Association of India (IAMAI) and IMRB's recent findings, with increasing affordability of PCs and internet penetration, India has 121 million internet users in December 2011. Out of 121 million, 97 million are expected to be active internet users. With this internet use in India is expected to enter a critical period of growth with the possibility of becoming the largest internet using country in the world in this decade. The Indians have witnessed the revolution in information and communication sectors and a qualitative transformation in social, economic and political sectors, mainly as a result of free flow of information and sharing of knowledge. Already, India has crossed the initial decades of IT revolution; the present decade is the most challenging for both the government and IT industry to provide cost-effective services of information highway, the internet, for the citizens to support and enable their prosperity, growth, challenge, and opportunities in domestic sectors.

To meet such an upsurge in media, more professional and skill-oriented persons are required. Also, these professionals need to be competent enough in their relevant fields. A professional degree holder can be of an added advantage in this scenario, giving an opportunity to the industry to exploit his capabilities in the competitive online journalism/media market. Besides, the range of work of a journalist demands different talents and temperaments, but all who aspire to adopt journalism requires some basic skills and attitudes such as wide-ranging interests, overall social awareness, an inquiring mind, punctuality, willingness to work hard, an initiative mind to understand the unspoken words, and also to read between the lines to perceive that is not directly revealed.

Journalism Education System

Though Indian journalism and mass communication education is seven decades old, it has yet to take an appropriate shape. In earlier days, journalism education meant only imparting skills and crafts in reporting, editing and newspaper production. After being neglected for a long time, journalism and mass communication courses in India are witnessing a lot of demand from students on pursuing their careers in media. Media education has now steadily assumed need-oriented, field-based, scientific-tested role reflecting dynamic modern needs, trends and varied testes of consumer and clients. The boom in private television channels and broadcasting organisations fuel the demand for this education.

The journalism education is recognised as professional education, usually referred to by different nomenclatures, viz., journalism, mass communication, advertising, public relations, and media studies depending on the emphasis on different aspects. One important aspect of these courses is that the students undergo rigorous training in the skills required for the profession. Over half of the total Indian university departments offering journalism courses are providing one-year diploma only and nearly one-fifth are providing bachelor's degree under varied course titles as Bachelor of Journalism, Bachelor of Journalism and Mass Communication, Bachelor of Mass Communication, Bachelor of Mass Communication and Journalism; and the masters programme as Master in Journalism and Mass Communication, Master in Communication, and Journalism, MA (Communication), Master in Science Communication (MSC), and M. ScC (Agricultural Communication). A few universities are offering full-time M.Phil. and doctoral programmes.

The syllabus of journalism studies taught at university level is varied, and in the recent past, advanced topics like broadcast communication, rural communication, agricultural communication, science communication and some special modules have been included in the course patterns. The growing number of science magazines and the attention paid to science by both the print and the broadcast media have resulted in the institution of programmes on science communication at the post-graduate level. Some universities like Berhampur University, Odisha, have also introduced journalism as a subject in pre-university degree level pass and honours programmes. Considering a growing relationship among industry, management, money/share market, and media, a new class of journalism, i.e., business journalism has taken birth.

A number of media houses also train some of their journalists/desk writers by selecting potential students with necessary skills and putting them through journalism training workshops and on-the-job training 'intern' programmes. Such media houses believe that they build employee loyalty and increases long-term employee retention rates while also proving cost-efficient. The Times Research Institute and Eenadu School of Journalism are the institutions that are the best examples. A few institutes like the Delhi-based Times Centre for Media Studies, Symbosis Institute of Management, etc. used to offer a course in business journalism to MBAs, CAs, post-graduates with good degrees in economics, commerce, marketing, social science, and having talent for writing.

Hurdles in the Education

The medium of Indian journalism and mass communication education is mainly English. A limited institutes and universities are offering diploma and degree courses in Hindi and other Indian vernacular languages. Except a very few, the universities and institutes offering courses in vernacular languages are limited to diploma level, but Hindi is an exception to this category. If one opts for higher education, there is no alternative to considering English as the only medium of education, which prevents many regional language media professionals from acquiring higher media education. It is believed that the other regional language education is hardly considered fruitful for this profession despite the fact that language press (e.g., *Malayala Manorama, Gujurat Samachar, Dainik Bhaskar*) has outnumbered the English press in terms of circulation and readership and has entered a new phase of development.

In India, the universities are mostly located in metros/cities and the journalism and communication courses offered by them do not emphasise on education or training necessary for a student to be a rural communicator. Also, most of the students, after completion of the course and because of aptitude and appropriate training for working as a communicator in urban areas, prefer placement in cities and towns where mass media establishments are located. The lack of rural communication-oriented education and training methods in journalism schools, and limited opportunities for rural communication practitioners have prevented them from making their profession as a social engineer in the society.

A common problem in a majority of journalism schools is the absence of full-time faculty. Even where full-time faculty exists in some of the journalism departments at university level, part-time teachers are still hired from the media organisations. The part-time teachers may be good in their field especially in practical aspects, but many a time it is found that they are not well conversant with theoretical aspects. This lacuna damages the interest of the students in the subject, as they are not exposed to the subject in an appropriate way. Though, sometimes, even the high-ranking full-time teachers also lack practical experience and they only depend on books and study material for their lectures. In India, communication educators prefer serving media industry to teaching profession mainly because the industry is a good paymaster. There is thus an urgent need for good, competent and inspired full-time faculty, having both theoretical and practical knowledge, to avoid most serious communication education problems the country is facing today.

As per the practice, most of the journalism and mass communication schools in India aim at producing students who could later be absorbed in the country's media establishments. The job requirements in the media establishments require the entrants to have some practical experience. The state of regional language media education has been inviting criticism from professionals and media establishments for several reasons. The media organisations also do not pay enough attention towards the growth of journalism education and find out ways to improve the existing situation. With the exception of a limited number of schools like the Indian Institute of Mass Communication, most of the journalism schools in India do not have proper facilities for training the students. The degree holders with inadequate training from journalism schools invite criticism from various quarters, which continues to mount. A majority of journalism departments in universities find it difficult to bring out a laboratory journal even once a year. Similar scenario also exists in the case of audio-visual media training centers. The rapidly changing situation in the development of the communication and the insufficient professional competency of pass out students and their fitness to work on the state-of-the art technical equipment is posing a great challenge in media sector.

In India, the journalism and mass communication research is still premature despite several studies. These include media's participation in electoral process, media consumption behaviour of people, media's impact on social, political, and cultural behaviour of people, etc. The main problem behind mass communication research in India is unavailability of literature for research survey. The UGC Report on the Status of Journalism and Mass Communication Education in India rightly pointed out, 'Communication research is an absolutely virgin field in Indian universities. It is more true in the case of university departments which cater mainly to the needs of the language press.' Actually, the press itself should take the initiative and start research, in collaboration with university departments to overcome these general deficiencies.

Besides all these above factors, another major one is the near absence of library facilities for students. Due to insufficient financial support from the university, the department unable to meet the requirements of the students to access to valuable books which are essential for up-to-date knowledge on modern communication methods. Old and western concept books are inappropriate for the present curriculum. This also results in the loss of enthusiasm among the students.

Redefining Course Curricula

Though the course curriculum of Indian journalism and mass communication education taught at various university levels have been changed significantly from western-oriented to Indian pattern still much efforts are needed to improve in this regard. Western methods of research and use of their books are still prevailing in our present education curriculum. It is a discouraging trend in Indian journalism. There is a strong need for a new curriculum, based on the philosophy of Indian culture, practices and values. The communication courses should aim at creating consciousness within communications circle. Development of skills and value-oriented syllabi and alternative teaching materials should be given high priority in the journalism and communication courses in Indian context.

Also, there is a need to follow a selective course structure as recommended by the UGC by all university journalism departments. Research-oriented subjects should be introduced in the course pattern, with subject specialisation like rural, agricultural, science, political, broadcast and electronic communication. The journalism departments should take advantage of the UGC projects in various fields and appoint the researchers. This may on one hand raise the employment opportunities and on the other help the students to acquire relevant practical knowledge. The faculty members should also take special interest in the field of research, publication of the research results and programmes for audio-visual media. All this can help explore ways by which an effective and participatory communication process be set up at different levels.

As already stated, most of the students aspire to work in metros in print and electronic media and show very little interest in rural and agricultural communication, though the latter has wider career opportunities. Each year, even less than one per cent of pass-outs engage themselves in interpersonal and culture-based communication. This is due to the lower weightage assigned to these areas at the study level. Though the course content contains topics on rural forms of mass communication, the lack of interest on the part of the teachers adversely affects the enthusiasm among the students.

There is a strong need for inclusion of training in the curricula to ensure relevance of the programme to the students in acquiring adequate levels of professional skills, with increased emphasis on social, political and economic aspects. This calls for a change in the education methods, in cooperation with various other departments like psychology, anthropology, and sociology. This will help in focussing attention on the purpose of a value-oriented journalism education.

Career Opportunities

Today's big business is keeping people informed and entertained. India is becoming an important entertainment and information hub in Asian subcontinent. It is not just in television broadcasting that India is attracting foreign investors but also the popularly of Hollywood movies has increased multifold as their dubbed versions have found a bigger market in India. Channels like Discovery and National Geographic are devoting prime time to the programmes dubbed in Hindi. Discovery has uncovered the Indian hunger for infotainment. Round the clock Indian news channels from Star News, Zee News, CNN-IBN, Times Now, News 24, India TV, BBC, CNN, etc., have opened up a big market for media professionals to provide more authentic and value-oriented Indian news and current affairs programmes.

There is also a huge swell in entertainment channels in India. Entertainment appears to be the fastest growing area. There are more cartoons, music video, soap operas, etc. than ever before. Satellite broadcasting and cable television have opened up enormous opportunities for TV producers of software. On the technical front, this has also resulted in the mushrooming of video studios with sophisticated equipment providing a range of services, and consequently providing career opportunities for those with technical training in this field. There is, therefore, an ongoing demand for radio, audio and video announcers, anchors, performers, singers, directors, producers, news readers/anchors, television journalists, photographers, cinematographers, art directors, set designers, costume/fashion designers, etc. for the umpteen television channels. Other jobs in this field include audio/video music recording, specialisations in sound and/or lighting for live and recorded programmes, design, manufacture and sales of hardware and software for entertainment, production of advertising commercials as well as areas such as interactive videos and teleconferencing.

In almost all its diversified fields, journalism education has a wide scope and plenty of career opportunities in our country. Rising trend of internet communication and online publishing in India has widened the scope for the journalism professionals. Web designers, creative technical writers, online editors are now in much more demand and employment opportunities are more than ever before. Seeing this potential emerging growth sector and the opportunities thereby, several universities and institutes have now started offering courses on software journalism. It is also being noticed that several computer teaching institutes have now started offering an additional course on technical writing to the software candidates which often led the professionals to establish their career in the field of technical writing, web editing, internet publishing, etc.

Global news is also transforming itself as a necessity. Since having their own people covering the globe is expensive, television channels are regularly exploring links with the local broadcasters, finding out if they can have reliable people locally. There are also some foreign radio stations like the BBC and Voice of America which have their representative offices in India, mainly for news, and employ newsreaders from time to time. There is in this search a huge opportunity for trained professionals to explore. Besides, the trained professionals can find jobs in government departments of All India Radio, Doordarshan and other allied sectors of the Ministry of Information and Broadcasting through Union Public Service Commission (UPSC) and Staff Selection Commission (SSC) selection.

Measures for Improving of Journalism Education

1. The present course pattern of journalism and communication should be made more interesting by providing sufficient exposure to the advanced technological innovations like computers, satellite, laser, informatics, and electronic delivery systems, so that the students may acquaint themselves with the nature of work in an ever-changing modern communication industry.
2. The internship training programme of about two months in the present course pattern at diploma/degree level is not sufficient. To gain practical knowledge in developing skills of a minimum standard, the training programme period should range from three to six months.
3. Relevance of social communication and the role of social communicator in the society should be given high priority, keeping in view its importance in a developing nation like India.
4. The University Grants Commission (UGC) guidelines with regard to recruitment of teachers in journalism and

communication should be reviewed. Besides, the present lectureship test clearance, a minimum of one-year experience in a media house with some research-oriented work should be included as essential qualifications for recruitment of journalism and communication teachers.

5. The western style and model of communication still being followed should be discouraged. The media teachers, social thinkers, and communication planners should prepare guidelines for journalism/communication education rooted in Indian culture. The UGC should support these efforts by preparing a syllabi common for all university journalism departments. The syllabi must give due attention to the regional and local journalism practices and communication methods.
6. The insufficient infrastructure in journalism departments affects the efficiency and standard of the students. There should be a minimum basic infrastructure for providing effective training leading to the development of skills, before introducing the programme. The UGC should also encourage those departments who have taken initiative on their own without getting any assistance from either the government or the UGC.
7. M.Phil. and doctoral programmes in journalism should be initiated at the universities to provide the students an opportunity for higher studies. This will help in the development of this field through research and development.
8. Media research centers should be opened in select universities so that the researchers get employment opportunities. This will also help the students gain in-depth knowledge and integrating ability to various frameworks of communication process.
9. The practical classes of journalism do not attract students for many reasons. To remedy this, the department must subscribe to some news agency, and skilled teachers should guide the students in editing and rewriting aspects of an agency copy. The department should install desktop publishing system and encourage the students to prepare their own laboratory journals, bulletins, etc. TV camera, VCR and tape-recorder are essential practical equipment for a student who takes the audio-visual subject as a specialisation. Good knowledge in handling and practical applications of these instruments is highly desirable. The university and the UGC should provide necessary equipment to all the journalism departments where audio-visual courses are offered.
10. The necessities of language media education must be reorganised in view of the growing figure of vernacular press and

readers' acceptance to this press, as it shapes their public opinion, provide large information, and generates awareness. The universities that are providing the education should concentrate more on the development of vernacular language education methods and improve the professional skills of the media practitioners. Reformative measures are needed in shifting the emphasis from English to vernacular language-oriented programmes, though a comprehensive measure is highly desirable.

11. A full-fledged course curriculum based on software/web journalism, technical writing, functions and uses of internet, web designing, and other allied areas should be appropriately adopted in the study curricula of all university journalism education system. This will help the professionals to get acquainted with the practical training before their employment.
12. Library facilities are generally poor in all university journalism departments. To overcome this problem, the UGC and the university should grant more financial assistance for library development, on priority basis.
13. Besides providing the usual education practice, the university and the UGC should conduct short-term correspondence and refresher courses for media persons and teachers to enable them to improve their ability in correlating the learning and its application in the workplace.
14. To meet emerging challenges in journalism education, the UGC and universities should take immediate steps to fill up the posts laying vacant for several years.
15. Special attention should be given by the journalism and communication departments to create employment opportunities for their products, as various management departments do. In this regard, the department should keep constant, live contact with media organisations and advertising and public relations agencies. Appropriate information regarding the scope and future prospects in various areas would enable the students to choose their lines as appropriately suited to them.
16. New media organisations and institutions of journalism education must initiate on the state of the research on media and publish the findings, leading to a body of original work in this field.
17. In the age of globalisation of media, a rounded media education be made part of the academic curriculum at the high school level, so that the youth of the country develop a critical awareness and perspective relating to news media and their role in the society.

18. University journalism departments and media institutions should approach working journalists and editors of newspapers and broadcasting channels, other professional associations and media industry bodies to enhance and intensify their interactions with students and researchers, discussions on media impact and other cooperative activities.
19. The recent decision of the government to constitute a task force to check the mushrooming growth of unregulated media institutes which charge exorbitant fees but provide sub-standard education, is a welcome step. This step would suggest measures to strengthen the media education and regulatory framework.

It is well considered that the media has an important role to play in minimising general deficiencies in our system of journalism and mass communication education. This requires a planned study, action and interchange of ideas among education systems and media organisations. As change is essentially a process at all levels, certain specific task-oriented proposals, agendas, and finally action frameworks be planned in a broad network to meet the challenges for the present and the future. If the planned framework does not meet the objectives, there is a chance of degradation of the journalism education. This ultimately will have an adverse affect on the quality of the media industry.

The present media boom in Indian market is a challenge to the efficiency and exposure of the trained journalistic products. Also, it is important for the trained products to preserve the culture and values. The role of journalists in social development in the upsurging media market needs to be evaluated urgently. To achieve social goals, both the role of the communication media and our system of communication education are equally important. There is also a need to reconstitute the present journalism and mass communication syllabus curriculum emphasising more on IT and its relevance to information age and allied areas. There should be a target by all of us who are more or less associated with the mass communication and journalism education and research activities in India to bring this a status equivalent with that of the other programmes in this seventy-one birth year. It is an opportunity and a challenge for Indian journalism and communication professionals to participate in global revolution in information systems and technological order and to leapfrog into the future if we can establish a strong action and result-oriented communication education and research system.

Changes

Journalism in India has undergone radical changes since economic reforms began in 1991. With the pronounced expansion of foreign and Indian electronic media into journalism, the landscape of journalism has expanded across all regions of India. In addition to the state-run All India Radio, there are nearly 450 television channels, 350 FM radio stations (with 10 service providers), 6,000 newspapers, 1,000 movies produced per year, 80 million pay-TV homes and 119 million television households. Mobile telephones with 26 spectra, the Internet, cable television and direct-to-home television (DTHTV) have enabled electronic media to reach 80-90% of the population, of which about 50-60% is rural, a phenomenon which both Sainath (2001) and Sonwalkar (2002) have referred to as the 'Murdochization of Indian Media'. The number of regional channels in all recognised Indian languages is also steadily increasing each year. In Andhra Pradesh alone, there are nearly 44 regional language television channels and 45 FM radio stations (by five major service providers) across the state. At the same time, there is an explosion of print media publications, with many newspapers being launched in regional languages, which Ninan (2007) described as a 'rural newspaper revolution'.

Common Modules in Communication and Journalism

S. No.	Course Module	Bachelor's Level	Master's Level	PG Diploma Level
1	Reporting and Editing	✓	✓	✓
2	Writing to Media	✓	✓	✓
3	Advanced Reporting	✓	✓	✓
4	Advertising	✓	✓	
5	Public Relations	✓	✓	✓
6	Television Production	✓	✓	
7	Radio Production	✓	✓	✓
8	Graphics and Animation	✓	✓	✓
9	Internet and Web Journalism	✓	✓	✓
10	Corporate Communication	✓	✓	✓
11	Media Ethics and Law	✓	✓	✓
12	Media Research	✓	✓	✓
13	Development Communication	✓	✓	✓

S. No.	Course Module	Bachelor's Level	Master's Level	PG Diploma Level
14	Documentary Production	✓	✓	✓
15	Film Production Studies	✓	✓	✓
16	Media History	✓	✓	✓
17	Communication Theory	✓	✓	
18	Magazine Journalism	✓	✓	✓
19	Photo Journalism	✓	✓	✓
20	Media Management	✓	✓	✓

Some Journalism Schools in India

- Asian College of Journalism
- Convergence Institute of Media Management and Information Technology Studies
- The Delhi School of Communication
- Haridev Joshi University of Journalism and Mass Communication
- Indian Institute of Mass Communication
- Indraprastha College for Women
- Jaganath International Management School
- Kushabhau Thakre PatrakaritaAvamJansancharVishwavidalaya
- Lingaya Lalita Devi Institute of Management and Sciences
- Makhanlal Chaturvedi National University of Journalism and Communication
- Manorama School of Communication
- MassCoMedia
- National Institute of Mass Communication and Journalism
- Press Academy of Andhra Pradesh
- School of Communication Studies, Punjab University
- Tecnia Institute of Advanced Studies
- Vivekananda Institute of Professional Studies

13 Fashion Designing Education

India is a country with an ancient clothing design tradition yet emerging in a modern fashion industry. Though a handful of designers existed prior to the 1980s, the late 80s and the 90s saw a spurt of growth. This was the result of increasing exposure to global fashion and the economic boom after the economic liberalisation of the Indian economy in 1990. The following decades firmly established fashion as an industry across India.

Post-Independence: Ethnic Revival and Bollywood Fashion

The history of clothing in India dates back to ancient times, yet fashion is a new industry, as it was the traditional Indian clothing with regional variations, be it the sari, ghaghra choli or dhoti, that remained popular until the early decades of post-independent India. A common form of Indian fashion originates from Western culture. A famous Indian fashion trademark is embroidery, an art of sewing distinct thread patterns. A way to include the traditional look and create a new fashion statement includes embroidery applied to different dresses, skirts, shirts, and pants to reflect the western culture influence as well as include the Indian tradition.

As part of larger revival movement in the Indian textile industry, Ritu Kumar, a Kolkata-based designer and textile print-expert started working on reviving the traditional hand block printing techniques of Bengal, and making it a part of the fashion industry, established "Ethnic Chic". She opened her first boutique in Delhi in 1966. In 1973, she first showcased the Zardozi embroidery in her garments, which had its origins in the royal costumes dating back to the Mughal era. This led to the revival of this lost art. Later embroidery became a prominent feature of Indian wedding attire, and also one of the country's biggest fashion exports. This was a period of revival, where various organisations, NGOs and individuals were involved in reviving traditional Indian techniques, in weaving, printing, dyeing, or embroidery, including ikat patola (double-ikat), bandhani (tie-dye) and shisha (mirror embroidery).

An early trendsetter in fashion was Bollywood (Hindi cinema), where costume designers like Bhanu Athaiya started experimenting with film fashion in the 1960s. Athaiya started working on period costumes in *Sahib Bibi Aur Ghulam* (1962) and *Amrapali* (1966), though she went on to introduce varied trends through *Teesri Manzil* (1966), *Chalte Chalte* (1976), *Karz* (1980) and *Chandni* (1989). These were soon followed by the mass market. Also situations and themes in Indian cinema became westernised, making way for the display of diverse fashion. Over the years, popular Bollywood trends have been the Madhubala's Anarkali-look with kurtas and churidars in *Mughal-e-Azam* (1960), purple embroidered sari worn by Madhuri Dixit in *Hum Aapke Hai Koun...!* (1994), to Rani Mukherji's short kurti-suits in *Bunty Aur Babli*(2005), *Veer Zaara* suits and blouses from *Parineeta*. This comes besides various fashion interpretations of the sari in films like *Chandni* (1989) with Sridevi, *Main Hoon Naa*(2004) with Sushmita Sen and *Dostana* (2008) with Priyanka Chopra, which became fashion trends.

However, in recent decades, with increasing exposure to the West, its influence is no longer as strong as in previous decades. By the 2003, with rise in the Indian diaspora around the world and the non-resident Indians, Bollywood continued to exert far greater influence on the fashion sensibilities amongst Indians around the world.

1980s and Fashion Boom

By the early 1980s, the first generation of Indian fashion designers started cropping up, including Satya Paul. However, it was Rohit Khosla (1958-1994) who became a pioneer in the fashion industry, when he co-founded "Ensemble" in 1987, with Tarun Tahiliani, Abu Jani-Sandeep Khosla and others. Though the "Anarkali-style" has been around ever since, it was first popularised after *Mughal-e-Azam* (1960). It was Abu Jani-Sandeep Khosla, who inspired by costumes of Mughal courtesans and Meena Kumari's costumes in *Pakeezah* (1975), introduced the floor-length Anarkali style of chudihar-kurta in 1988, which soon became the Indian version of the ball gown.

In 1986, the Ministry of Textiles, Government of India opened the National Institute of Fashion Technology (NIFT) in Delhi with the help of the Fashion Institute of Technology, New York. It played an important role in bringing in locally trained fashion designers. By 2010, it had developed 15 branches across India, and smaller private fashion institutions had also developed. Also in 1987, Tarun Tahiliani and his wife Shailja Tahiliani, founded "Ensemble", India's first multi-designer boutique in Mumbai.

In 1990, economic liberalisation of the Indian economy took place, which also propelled the fashion industry. In the following decade, fashion industry experienced a boom, both in terms of volume and trends. Designer Suneet Varma, inspired by his training in France, introduced an Indo-western, metal breast plate, followed by the "corset blouse" in 1992, made with satin, polyester taffeta or stretch lace. It was designed to replace the traditional choli, or Indian blouse worn with a sari in its early years, the 1980s, Indian design largely focused on *haute couture*; however, in the next decade, India saw a growth in the domestic retail industry, as well as an influx of outsourced garment business from the western countries. This meant better quality and larger manufacturing facilities available locally. Together, these reasons spurred many Indian designers to start their lines.

"God-printed T-shirts" were introduced by Manish Arora in 1997. Another important reinvention was made in 1998 by Monisha Jaisingh, who shortened the traditional Kurta to develop the Kurti, which became popular worldwide as the "Indian embroidered tunic". Also in the same year, the Fashion Design Council of India was established, which later started the India Fashion Week in Delhi, to promote Indian designers and manufacturers. In 2000, another Bollywood costume designer, Manish Malhotra, became an important influence on Indian fashion. Having designed the trendy looks for actresses Urmila Matondkar in *Rangeela* (1995) and Karisma Kapoor in *Raja Hindustani* (1996), he introduced the "cocktail sari" in 2000. Using pastel colours, and fabrics like chiffon, satin or net, he revived the traditional sari in a modem avatar. He was in turn inspired by the popular Bollywood saris of the 1960s and the chiffon saris worn by the actress in Yash Chora films, like *Chandni* (1989). This also started another era of Bollywood fashion influence and its collaboration with leading designers, besides leading actors and actresses occasionally walking the ramp for some designers.

By 2009, the Indian fashion industry, despite the ongoing recession, was worth ₹12.9 billion (US$41 million). Also in the same year,

Manish Arora, known for his quirky-kitsch became the first Indian designer to participate in Paris Fashion Week.

10 Facts about the Fashion Industry

1. It's not just about Fashion Designers

The fashion industry in India, just like in any other country is also about fashion photography. pattern making, garment construction, accessory designing, make-up artists, modelling, fabric weaving, textile research and development, fashion journalism/editorial, and manufacturing to name a few.

Fashion designers are just a small portion of this whole game. In India, other sectors like manufacturing fabric, importing and exporting textiles, embroidery and dyeing make up a much bigger proportion of this industry.

2. Fashion Industry Statistics

Current size of the Indian fashion industry is worth ₹1000 crore, while the market size is approximated to be ₹20,000 crore.

However, Indian fashion accounts for a meagre 0.2% in the world market. But this is expected as Indian fashion has just rolled over from infancy to the growth stage.

The signs are everywhere growing number of designers, boutiques and outlets, design schools and customers.

3. Not a Career for the Academically Challenged

It is only getting tougher and tougher to get into the National Institute of Fashion Technology (NIFT), the premier fashion institute in India. Fashion has its own technology. The myth is that Fashion is all about art. Fashion, when it actually comes down to sewing a dress, is actually Maths.

If you were bad at geometry in school, forget enjoying fashion designing. NIFT has tough aptitude tests for entrance exams, and it is highly competitive. Fashion is not meant (supposedly) for the back-benchers or the D-graders in school.

4. The Unorganised Industry

Continuing from the point above, the numbers are so low only because much of the industry is really unorganised.

Much of this trade goes unaccounted for. There are many NGOs which harness the talent of underprivileged women to make delightful accessories and bags, but this is rarely considered as fashion.

If you decide to start up your own home boutique, that also would go into the unorganised part, and would rarely reflect in the industry's profitable nature.

5. Famous Indian Designers

Ritu Verma, Rohit Bal, Manish Malhotra, Sabyasachi: these are names that not only you and I know but are famous international names.

If they could do it, then anyone else can do it. Their design sensibilities draw from Indian traditions and they have played an important part in showcasing our culture to the world.

Even with modernity thumping on the doors, many Indian designers find a way to weave in traditional ethos into their costumes and that is one reason why Indian fashion remains unique.

6. The Saree covers more ground than you think

If I asked you which sold most in India: Kurtas, Sarees or Denim, you would be amazed that Saree is the highest selling fashion apparel. It trumps all other kinds of styles by a very large margin and continues to grow at 8.8%. The sheer volume of sarees sold here will leave you spell-bound and the business done in these bustling hubs will make your jaw drop.

7. Fashion and Sleaze

Well, maybe Bollywood is sleazy. Just because they made a movie "*Fashion*" which was supposed to depict the Indian Fashion industry, does not mean the entire industry functions that way.

8. Made in India

Not only is India one of the largest exporter of textiles and clothes but many foreign countries set up their manufacturing units here: Gap Inc & Tommy Hilfiger to name a few.

Due to the cheap labour here and other Asian countries, you are bound to see that all the high-end international clothes are indeed made here. So basically, such international brands are easily able to sell at 400% margin.

Unfortunately for us, all the best quality fabrics are used for goods that are meant to be exported and the clothes that remain in India are often of poorer or cheaper quality.

9. Silk and Cotton

We are the second largest producer of Silk (after China) and third largest producer of Cotton. With such a background and surplus, it is only natural that most of our fashion would use these fabrics.

It is heart-warming to see all the designers of our generation bringing back the humble Khadi and handloom fabrics, innovated to suit our tastes. Khadi/Cotton is our pride.

10. Bright Prospects for the Fashion Industry, but a Long Way to Go

So all said and done, India still has a long way to go in carving a niche for itself in the world's fashion scene.

In terms of quality, in terms of talent, the research and innovation, we still have much to prove.

There's a long way to go before we can discover our confident and comfortable space.

Top Fashion Designing Colleges (2018)

1. NIFT, Delhi
2. NIFT, Navi Mumbai
3. NIFT, Bengaluru
4. Pearl Academy, Delhi
5. NIFT, Chennai
6. NIFT, Kolkata
7. NIFT, Patna
8. NIFT, Hyderabad
9. NIFT TEA College Knitwear Fashion, Tiruppur
10. NIIFT, Mohali
11. Pearl Academy, Jaipur
12. NIFT, Bhubaneswar
13. School of Fashion Technology, Pune
14. Vogue Institute of Fashion Technology, Bengaluru
15. Army Institute of Fashion and Design, Bengaluru
16. Amity School of Fashion Technology, Noida
17. NIFT Kannur
18. Symbiosis Institute of Design, Pune
19. JD Institute of Fashion Technology, Mumbai
20. Rachana Sansad, Mumbai.

Admission Process for the Top 20 Colleges

- One can apply to the college through their NIFT Entrance Exam or other University level Exam conducted by the authority.
- Applying must fullfil all the required eligibility criteria made under the admission guidelines.

Eligibility Criteria

Programme	Eligibility	Age Limit
Bachelor of Design - B.Des.: (Fashion Design. I/Leather Design / Accessory Design / Textile Design / Knitwear Design / Fashion Communication)	The aspirant must have the XIIth I level examination in the 10+2 pattern of examination of any recognized Central/ State Board of Secondary Examination, such as Central Board of Secondary Education/State Board New Delhi, and Council for Indian School of Certificate Examination, New Delhi. or General Certificate Education (GCE) Examination (London/Cambridge/ Sri Lanka) at the Advanced (A) level/ International Baccalaureate (IB). or Any Public School/Board/University Examination in India or foreign countries recognised by the Association of Indian Universities as equivalent to 10+2 system. or A passing grade in the Senior Secondary School Examination conducted by the National Open School with a minimum of Five ' subjects.	Maximum age limit 23 years The upper age limit may be relaxed by a period of 5 (five) years for the candidates of Scheduled Castes/Scheduled Tribe/Person With Disability (PWD)

National Institute of Fashion Technology

Established in 1986 under the aegis of the Ministry of Textiles, Government of India and in collaboration with Fashion Institute of Technology, New York (FIT), National Institute of Fashion Technology (NIFT) is India's premier fashion school and a pioneer in design, management, and technology education related to the fashion industry in the region.

Over the last three decades, the institute has set academic benchmarks, excelled in thought leadership, and enabled its students to assume leadership positions in fashion businesses in India and overseas.

NIFT's undergraduate programmes include

B.Des. (Bachelor of Design-Fashion)
B.Des. (Bachelor of Design-Textiles)
B.Des. (Bachelor of Design-Knitwear)
B.Des. (Bachelor of Design-Accessories)
B.Des. (Bachelor of Design-Leather)
B.Des. (Bachelor of Design-Fashion)

B.F Tech (Bachelor of Fashion Technology-Apparel Production)

NIFT's postgraduate programmes include
M.Des. (Master of Design)
M F M (Master of Fashion Management)
M F Tech. (Master of Fashion Technology)

National Institute of Fashion Technology (NIFT) Embarks on a New Journey

As aspiring students of design throng, the 16 NIFT centers, that are busy hosting Open House sessions for interactions and counseling, it is imperative for parents and candidates to know what's new at NIFT. This premier design institute restructurs its curriculum after careful review and deliberations. This has been done to make students more industry ready and prepared to successfully manage the dynamic, complex world of fashion technology, design and retailing.

The curriculum now integrates technical know-how with soft skills, creativity with entrepreneurship, and education with exploration. The new curriculum at NIFT will equip the students with an extraordinarily valuable set of skills required for a well-rounded personality that can tackle the rigors of a fast-paced professional environment. It does so, by teaming a host of general electives, inter disciplinary minors, and deepening specialisations with the majors. From 2019 onwards, NIFT has also introduced a diverse range of general electives that include niche areas like Theatre, Psychology, Critical Thinking, Professional Ethics, among others. Adapting to the changing times, it has also incorporated technology-centric areas like Artificial Intelligence, Internet of Things, Big Data and Business Analytics, Smart Textiles and Smart Jewellery, into the curriculum. NIFT is optimistic that this will encourage more candidates with specialised and distinct interest areas to apply for its programmes.

In addition to this, the Institute has firmly integrated the Craft Cluster Initiative into its new curriculum. This, it is believed, will inspire students to draw from our country's rich and diverse cultural heritage, arts and crafts and metamorphose and assimilate the learnings into the current trends and requirements of the fashion industry and the society at large.

NIFT intends to deploy innovative pedagogy, in the form of academic transaction, opportunities for interdisciplinary learning and specialisation, assimilative and continuous evaluation and academic mention-ship to give student a holistic understanding of subjects, contexts, environment and an ability to adapt and innovate.

The dynamic NIFT faculty and industry experts with hands-on experience, will teach the ambitious curriculum. The NIFT programme will give students firsthand exposure to the working of the industry and experience of some of its most seasoned practitioners. It will give the students the opportunity to take up classroom projects which respond to an industry brief, and to do industry internships under the mentorship of some of the best minds in the business.

NIFT has also been working towards expanding its global presence through international partnerships, student exchanges and participation in international seminars and symposia that allow for world class academic discourse and knowledge transfer. Students of all NIFT campuses will get the opportunity to join international twinning programmes depending on their academic performance.

With such world-class infrastructure, faculty opportunities for exposure, NIFT is ready to revolutionise design and fashion education in India.

Top Colleges in India for Fashion Designing

1. National Institute of Fashion Technology (NIFT), Delhi
2. Vogue Institute of Fashion Technology, Bengaluru
3. Pearl Academy of Fashion, Delhi
4. School of Fashion Technology, Pune
5. Symbiosis Institute of Design, Pune
6. National Institute of Design, Ahmedabad
7. International Institute of Fashion Design, Chandigarh

Top Colleges in Abroad for Fashion Designing

1. Central Saint Martin
2. Royal College of Arts
3. Persons, the School for Design
4. Kingston University
5. Ecole De La Chambre Syndicale
6. LA Cambre
7. Bunka Fashion College

References

Agriculture Education Day: ICAR. *www.icar.org*

Ananda Krishnan, M. (2007). New Directions in the Context of Globalisation. *The Indian Journal of Technical Education*, 30(1)

Basavanthappa, BT (2004). *Nursing Education.* New Delhi: Jaypee Brothers

Bendrow, I. (1998).*The Bases of Competence Skills for Lifelong Learning and Employability.* San Francisco: Jossy Bass

Bhargava, A. (2019). Casteism in a Medical College: A Reminiscence. *Indian Journal of Medical Ethics,* 2019.

Crawfort, D.G. (1914). *History of the Indian Medical Services: 1600-1913.* London: Thacker & Co

Dasgupta, S. (2014). Reforms in Medical Education: Optimising Quantity and Quality. *Indian Journal of Public Health*

Deo, MG (2009). Need for Research Oriented Medical Education in India. *IJMR*, 130(2)

Engineering education in India. *Shodhganga.inflibnet.ac.in*

Goel, C. and Goel, D. (2019). Teacher Education in India: Issues and Concerns. *University News,* 52(23)

Govt. of India (2019). Ministry of Ayush. *http://ayush.gov.in*

Govt. of India (2008). National Health Profile. *www.cbhidghs.nic.in*

Gupta, D. (2015). Teacher Education Curriculum in the Context of ICT. *Issues and Ideas in Education, 3(2)*

Gupta, A. (2004). *A Study of Existing Perception/Understanding of Education for Sustainable Development of Indian Teachers.* Lucknow: Prithvi Innovations

Guskey, T.R. and Huberman, A.M. (1995). *Professional Development in Practices: New Paradigm and Practices.* New York: Teachers College Press.

Guru, B.P.M. and Madhura, V.M.L. (2005). Journalism Education in India: A Quality Perspective. *www.What is India.com*

Indian Fashion Industry: *Economic Times,* 25-7-2009

Indian Nursing Council. *www.indian nursing council.org*

Karan, K. (2001). Journalism in India. *Journalism Studies, 2(2)*

Kumar, R. (2014). Media Education in India: An Introspection. *Indian Journal of Public Administration* 60(146-5)

Kuldova, T. (2016). *Luxury Indian Fashion.* London

Kumar, A. and Ambrish (2015). Higher Education: Growth, Challenges and Opportunities. *International Journal of Arts, Humanities and Management Studies,* 1(2)

Kumar, R. (2019). The Tyranny of the MCI's New MBBS Curriculum. *Journal of Med Prime Cave,* 2019(8)

Kumar, S. (2004). Report Highlights Shortcomings in Private Medical Schools in India. *British Medical Journal,* 328:90

Mahal, A. and Mohanam, M. (2006). Growth of Private Medical Education in India. *Medical Education,* 40(10)

Majumdar, A.A., D'Souza and Rahman, S. (2004). Trends in Medical Education: Challenges and Directions for Need Based Reform in South East Asia. *Journal of Medical Service,* 58(368)

Medical Education Policyand Medical Education. *http://mohfw.gov.in*

Mellor, J. (2011). International Journey of Agriculture Education. *Economic and Political Weekly,* 46(4)

Mukhopadahyay, M. (2006). *Total Quality Management in Education. New Delhi: Sage Publications.*

Salma N. and Noorain, A. (2011). Problem of Teacher Education in India. *International Referred Journal,* 2(19)

Suranjan Das (2007). The Higher Education in India and the Challenges of Globalisation. *Social Scientist,* 35(34)

Muppidi, S.R. (2008). Journalism in India. *Media Asia.* 35 (2)

Nagraj, K.V. (2020). Fragmented Media Topas of Professionalism in India. *CEMCA News Letter,* 6(1)

Naayak, R.K. and Devi, G. (1990). Code of Professional Ethics in Education. *www. academia.edu*

Nida, B. (2008). Teacher's Perception Levels of Activities Directed Towards Professional Progress. *Education,* 130

NCTE (2010). *National Curriculum Framework for Teacher Education towards Preparing Professional and Humane Teacher.* New Delhi.

Patnaik, S.N. (2002). *Sixty Years of Journalism Education – Prospects and Problems.* Ministry of I&B, Government of India, New Delhi.

Pawan Agarwal (2005). Engineering Education in India: Changing Global Realities and Responses. *University News,* 43(39)

Rao, PLV (2010). Journalism Education and Media Revolution. *Vidura,* 2(3).

Rajanna, M.V. (2017). Educational Transformation: What B-Schools can give to Business? *University News,* 53(50).

Saha, K.C. (1991). Reorienting Management Education. *Economic and Political Weekly,* 26(48)

Satyanarayana, P. and Lakshmi Mantha (2018). Management Education in India *University News,* 56(20)

Singh, A. (2005). Restructuring Medical *Education, Economic and Political Weekly,* 40(34)

Singh, T., Gupta, P., Singh, D. (2013). *Principles of Medical Education.* New Delhi: Jaypee Brothers

UNESCO (1996). *Learning: The Treasure Within* – Report of the International Commission on Education to UNESCO for the Education to UNESCO for the 21st Century. Paris: UNESCO

UNESCO (2007). Model Curricula for Journalism Education. *www.unesco.org*

Vijay Kumar (2008). Business Schools in India: Current Challenges and Future Opportunities. *Decision Line, (October 2008)*

Wilkinson, A. (1958). *A Brief History of Nursing in India and Pakistan.* Delhi: Trained Nurses Association of India